THE GAME
REVISITED

Stuart Roy Clarke

with

John Williams
University of Leicester

*In putting together this book I asked myself of each page
'Will this make you smile?'*

Foreword

BY HUNTER DAVIES

.

The Moon's a Balloon or is it a ball ? Strange how so many shapes in nature, on earth and in the heavens, are round, sort of circular, a bit like a ball. I like to think people on this planet have been playing football, in some form, of some sort, since well, people were on the planet, even if they were just kicking a roundish object around, a stone, a fruit, a lump of something, a pig's bladder, a bag of skin.

A pity Stuart Roy Clarke was not around earlier, to capture those early versions of the football game, but he has rather made up for it in these last forty years, observing football playing, football following, football loving, football influences, with an eye, imagination and sensitivity which no other football photographer in my long-legged experience has ever bettered.

I first came across him about thirty years ago, in Lakeland. I was driving through Ambleside, which has an ingenious one-way system, making it hell to stop, and I saw this sign saying: HOMES OF FOOTBALL. It appeared to be over some sort of shop front. But what could he be selling, what was he offering? Some mistake, surely. I must have miss-read the signs. It probably said HOME OF KENDAL MINT CAKE or HOMES OF CUMBERLAND RUM BUTTER. Next time I drove that way, I slowed down and discovered that I had read it correctly after all. But it still made little sense. How on earth can anything in Ambleside ever be a home of football? It is in the heart of Lakeland, miles from any industrial area, the traditional birthplace of most football clubs.

Alas, today the whole county of Cumbria has only one Football League club, the world famous Carlisle United. We did have another two, when I was a lad, Workington Town and Barrow, but they are currently slightly below the salt, off the edge of the table, not quite over the abyss but a bit out of national sight in the lower leagues, though naturally they will come back and zoom up the Football League.

Eventually, I managed to properly stop and investigate. The Homes of Football turned out to be more of a museum, a series of photographic displays and arrangements by a guy called Stuart Roy Clarke. Entry free, but of course you could buy prints and postcards. Over the years I bought loads of his postcards, eagerly awaiting his next endeavours. I loved every one. I don't think I have seen a boring, or bad, or dull Stuart Roy Clarke football image. They make me smile, because many are so witty; or they make me feel sad, looking at those poor sods trudging home in the rain having been stuffed once again. Or they make me think, because so often Stuart finds an oblique angle for a well-known football ritual, such as kick off, or even the teams lining up.

One thing about football, something which makes it so loved across the world, is that when you go to a game you feel you are communing with everyone or anyone who has ever played or ever gone to a game, anywhere, at any time, since the laws, as we still know them, were first defined in 1863. Where the game is taking place, the language, the climate, the terrain, are all irrelevant. You understand what is going on, how everyone feels.

At any game, amateur kick-about or professional match, I like to think that I am experiencing what people in the past have experienced – and will experience again in the future. We are all members of the football family. And Stuart Roy Clarke is our archivist, recording our family fun and our deepest soulful, heartfelt football feelings. Long may he continue to do so.

Chapters

Partnered By

And thanks to

Introduction

Stuart Roy Clarke (**SRC**) and University of Leicester Associate Professor in Sociology John Williams (**JW**) have known each other for 30 years.

While Stuart has been taking and exhibiting photographs of football stadia and the people in and around the game during that time, John has been writing about football and the fans who watch it for academic journals and books.

This is their first collaboration. The conversations which follow took place in Leicester in 2017 and 2018, bringing about the book THE GAME. Enthused about what they had produced and thinking the book had not gone far enough, once it had sold out they have added a further conversation and photographs for 2019. They have been specially edited for this volume THE GAME REVISITED. These conversations are designed to explore the history of football in Britain, the people who made it, and the role of photography in extending our understanding and enjoyment of a sporting activity and obsession that says so much about who we are as a people. We hope you enjoy reading them as much as we did kicking around ideas about the roots and meaning of the sport for the British.

CHAPTER 1

And Fate Handed Us The Ball

SRC: Let's begin at the beginning. I like to think of the coming of football as like a great meteorite hitting the earth. We couldn't really avoid it. *Boom!* Like it happened in one day and the game was almost waiting to be played on this planet since it started spinning. There is something metaphysical about why we all play the game, surely. Look at the ball's organic, natural shape. Circular forms like this have been worshipped, cared for, and kicked around since before records began, and well before the coming of photographic evidence. *Fate handed us the ball.*

Football was always going to happen: it was just a question of when and where... and how it would be played. England and that northern part of it where I have lived for so long, Cumbria, where Hunter Davies first came across me, claims it as *theirs*. Being even more specific, one could locate the epicentre of the original football arousal in that stoic old place of Workington, out there on the Cumberland coast. Perhaps Workington is to football what Windsor is to the monarchy. The difference being nobody goes to the *working-town* to discover this.

JW: Is it significant that we have some impressive early examples of local 'folk' football matches surviving today? Some go back a few hundred years and others – like your Workington example – much longer. You seem to have made a beeline for them with your camera, to include them alongside the more marketable, familiar and modern versions of the game.

SRC: I can't escape it: 'primitive' football is all around me it seems – in Cumbria where they have 'Uppies & Downies' and then, lo and behold, when I moved to Derbyshire there was the more celebrated Royal Ashbourne game 'Uppards & Downards' again on my doorstep. I would say to anyone 'COME ALONG! You will know as much about this as me; it's all played out in front of us'.

'Ball On The Village Green' - Elsdon, Northumbria, 2000
(SRC)

After all, these earthy sporting battles which some people may even think of as barbaric, are SO simple: you either play for the team going *UP*, or their counterparts going *DOWN*. There are no clear sides – anyone can play for anyone – at Workington it's traditionally Colliers kicking uphill, versus Sailors kicking down.

In the early 1800s, at places around Sheffield, a city which has claims to be the cradle of the modern game, sides were based on distinctions such as married men versus not-married-men. Today it may be married men versus divorced men. Or women. Anyhow, what I am trying to put across is that it's not a far cry from those jumpers-for-goalposts and school playground games where two captains pick their team based on who they like and don't like, preference for bigger kids, whatever. I am telling you this because no one ever goes there (Workington) to find out.

'Hand Crafted With Honour' - Uppies & Downies, Workington, 2015
(SRC)

JW: I like the fact that some of the young guys who play in these Uppies v Downies football contests in a handful of places up and down the country wear football shirts drawn from today's professional clubs, giving some connection to the modern game. They play not for reward, but rather for bragging rights. Or even for something we, the general population, can't quite grasp because it is now such a rare experience – playing for our people. However, I do get the feeling that in a world of branding and tourist this-and-that, there is something quite refreshing surely in this media-free zone.

SRC: Imagine it: it's Easter-time. We are back at Workington. An hour to kick-off. There is NO crowd and certainly nobody buying or selling tickets; then a trickle of people turns into a flood. They are all locals. You would not be surprised to see Boudicca arrive on a chariot bearing THE Ball. It's a soft leather cherished thing stitched (and what an honour to do so) by a local craftsman. It will be kicked, thumped, crushed under the weight of hefty blokes. It must NOT burst or have its innards fall out. Here the game takes as long as it takes – people go home, return to base (some players are on ASBOs), make an egg and bacon sandwich, have a kip, awake with love bites or to domestic disputes, walk the dog… then get back out there looking for the game they left hours ago. It could be anywhere around town.

This game that always starts in the light is invariably pitched into complete darkness for much of it – and it's hard to see the ball. Which could lead to abuse. Where, for hundreds of years there were categorically NO rules in the Workington game, they recently introduced just

one: you can't put the ball in a car and drive off. Because someone did.

But make no mistake, there's honour among 'no rules'. The players have their own code of conduct – they have to, as there are no referees, no commentators and the police stand well clear. There is practically no press coverage nor post-match analysis, save for pub talk.

JW: Theories abound about how we eventually moved on from the local versions of this wild Workington game, played on the land, across rivers and in the streets with no written rules. How did we get from here to modern football, with a specified number of players per side, an agreed pitch size and markings, and a more civilised and 'fair' approach to playing sport?

'One Or The Other' - Uppies & Downies, Workington, 2015
(SRC)

SRC: How convenient it would be if we could just say that after the shambolic sprawling rabble-rousing street matches, working-class people militantly, yet lovingly, set up factory clubs and organised their own teams. Indeed, this is what I thought was the universal truth when I was growing up. This was because our local youth football leagues around Watford were dominated by canny Scots who had come south mainly from Lanarkshire, to find work in modern factories such as Atlas Copco, Lucas Aerospace, Kodak, etc. And in my mind these men saw the *fitba'* as an area in their lives where they could take control, boss it, do something meaningful outside of work and – being good organisers – they could create a legacy for their bairns and for the bairns of others like them.

'Can't Be Put In A Car' - Uppies & Downies, Workington, 2015
(SRC)

JW: Respect is due to the Scots who so informed your youth, who did indeed produce so many organisers and managers of the game, but football's narrative is even more fascinating and more complicated than any one story.

Some historians argue that the English public schools and ex-schoolboys produced written rules for the handling and kicking games and then tried to spread them among working class people around Britain.

Others argue that in places such as East Lancashire, Sheffield and the Midlands, working people had already produced their own organised football culture and had devised local rules. They would soon recruit and pay working class Scottish 'professors', maestros of the feet and early natural team players, to advance the game and their local clubs.

SRC: Perhaps the two teams of historians should have a match to decide who is right!

JW: From 1863, the men who formed the world's first Football Association in London slowly began to exert national control by ironing out regional differences and producing a simple set of written laws that all supporters of the kicking game could understand. 'Hacking' would have to go - to the rugby field. We eventually had a national game to take to the world.

The game soon produced its early star performers. The professional version wasn't far away. Football, in evolutionary terms, just *had* to evolve and spread - it couldn't always be based on local bragging rights and on playing in the style of 'what used to be.'

SRC: The great Bill Shankly used to say about football: 'All you need is the sky, a ball and the grass'. Or no grass. Some of my earliest football memories are about images of working class footballers - Ashington's Bobby and Jackie Charlton - back in the fifties, playing with local kids in northern backstreets and alleyways. They did their stuff on knee-bruising concrete or cobbles. Shankly understood what football meant to his local pit village but he could also see how the simple game could touch everyone's lives. He was a native scientist AND a captain and a manager. He applied nuclear fission to football. *Bill split the football atom!*

By the 1960s monochrome had turned into colour in every home. At the moment that the human race was reaching for the stars with a space programme (which wasn't just a match between the Old Firm of the USA and Russia), Scotland had produced a truly great Celtic team. Even Northern Ireland showcased George Best, a man from a different planet. British football now seemed fuelled by a genuinely optimistic mood that everything might be possible and could be reached for.

'Football Kit Of Sorts' - Uppies & Downies, Workington, 2015
(SRC)

JW: I suspect this is not the last we'll hear about George. He was his own shooting star and, in some ways, he helped create the landscape for today's moneyed version of global football. The young Best certainly drove colour into the English game and he drove his various managers to distraction while doing it. Your enthusiasm for George strikes me as part of the paradox of your work: that on the one hand you want to record 'the Best effect', football reaching for the stars. But on the other, many of your

Manchester United footballer George Best shows manager Sir Matt Busby
his European Footballer of the Year Award at Old Trafford, 1969
(Mirrorpix)

photographs are so down to earth they also excavate its deep roots, the part that has little celebrity or glamour. You enjoy those tribal players of Workington, none of whom are star material, playing their dirty street game. But when the all-singing-all-dancing Premier League comes along, you want to embrace that too.

Your photographs show us that ALL are welcome in the football pleasure-dome. It is part of the enduring beauty and intrigue of fandom and football that they work so well on so many different levels.

SRC: The ball being that one thing that they all have in common. For me, the whole darned world is a football pitch – and football values are never very far away.

Look at that aerial view of Hackney Marshes and its 88 pitches. If not God Himself, then a god of football is surely looking down on this sporting landscape. The marshes are the grand epitome of the sort of place where, all over the country, young guys still do their regular Sunday morning battle. A player might boot the ball up-field not realising it's the ball from the pitch next door: two balls on the field. Scowling and laughing ensue. All part of the dualism of the game.

JW: Hackney Marshes does look like a vast geometric homage to pleasure and play. It is an extreme example. It is the altar of the grassroots game (albeit built on bomb damaged rubble). Anyone can play.

Hackney
Marshes in 1987, built
on marsh filled with
bombed building rubble
after World War 2
(Mirrorpix)

The 1957-58 Burnt Ash football team in Bromley - David Jones,
before he became Bowie, is seated on the far left
(Courtesy of Burnt Ash Primary School)

SRC: There is a lovely school team photo from the late-fifties involving, unlikely as this might seem, David Bowie. It reminds us that most British boys probably played some sort of football back then. It's the kind of memento that lots of men in Britain of a certain age will have in a box in the attic, on discreet show somewhere, or else locked away safely. I know yours, John, is above your downstairs toilet cistern! You see it every time you flush. Photographs like these are elegiac, reminding you of the passing of the years. Chalking the year on the ball locates the image time-wise, but it also gives the picture a kind of timeless quality.

JW: Sadly, local schools playing football – my toilet photo – seems to have got lost in this country. Most kids in state schools today will probably never get to experience that amazing feeling of representing your school at football.

In the 1960s in Liverpool, where the locals could lay claim to the game itself, as junior school kids if we had a match to play in the evening we could wear our tangerine football shirts to school, under our jumpers. Very proud we were. We had some tough rivalries: Protestant schools (that orange connection) taking on our Catholic nemeses. I guess we did come together, become a sort of Liverpool united, when we played representative matches against the Manchester schools.

SRC: For me, this is an essential part of the tribal nature of the game. You always need identifiable rivals – invaders –

to make it work best. It was those local rivalries that made the early forms of folk football so brutal and which gives the game an edge today, and probably will do tomorrow.

JW: Yet the beauty of organised football is that you can never entirely play your own game; you always have to take account of the opposition. The national team didn't always seem to get that message. When England lost 1-0 to the USA in the 1950 World Cup, some British journalists back home reported the result as 10-1 to England! They couldn't believe the score-line and assumed it was a mistake.

I suppose every cloud has a silver lining. Those recurring England losses in the early 1950s eventually led to the lifting of the maximum wage for players in the Football League in 1961. They also accelerated the debate about the need to reward and prepare British players properly – pay them for what was their profession, the thing they did best, much better than you or me, their livelihood. The new pay deal suddenly meant that some rising young stars like George Best could – at least for a short while in his case – really live the high life.

SRC: The British footballing jean-genie was finally out of the box.

CHAPTER 2

Teams of Eleven-A-Side

JW: Why does football have 11 players a side? Could we ever really know why? Eleven may sound like an arbitrary number, though with a lonely goalkeeper it does offer a bit of symmetry out on the pitch: five and five on each side of the field. It could also be something to do with the optimum number of players given the chosen pitch size. But it's probably something both more obvious and more complicated.

SRC: That other, rather boring, English game, that summer vision in white, had 11-a-side well before football took hold.

JW: Cricket is certainly the older sport and it did have 11 players a side – a balance of five batsmen and five bowlers, plus an extra player to keep wicket (cricket's goalkeeper) and to ensure that everyone had a chance to bat. Many early football teams were formed to keep cricketers fit during the winter. Sheffield and also Hallam FC, two of the world's first football clubs, grew up like this. Local men such as Nathaniel Creswick and William Prest in Sheffield helped produce its own local rules before the national FA laws were devised in 1863. But even these clubs out in the northern provinces were probably influenced, at some level, by public schoolboys returning to the sticks with a lofty vision of how to organise sport for the less privileged. The good men of Sheffield first drew up stumps and only when the dark nights set in did they take to kicking a football.

SRC: So, early football clubs were often reliant on your 'boring' old cricket to get started.

JW: When the early winter game eventually split into three different codes – association football, rugby league and rugby union – this produced different numbers of

A 2nd Division 'team of all the talents' - Sunderland had beaten Leeds United to win the FA Cup, year 1973
(Mirrorpix)

players for each code: 11, 13 and 15, respectively. The handling split came in 1871, when the Rugby Football Union was formed. But the rugby men were themselves two tribes. The working-class league professionals, who were based in a corridor across the north of England, went their own way in 1895, with upper class union amateurs dominating in other parts of the north and the south/west. Different again, Wales tried hardest to maintain rugby union as a sport for all classes. Both rugby codes wanted their version of football to be different from each other and their Association rival. So, they clutched their oval ball close to their chests and played the numbers game.

SRC: For me, 11-a-side football is still *the* game; not five, or seven, or the nine-a-side stuff. Whilst I get it that fielding smaller football teams allows everyone to have a touch, I get irritated these days by all the formats and different numbers of players playing football. If it's not eleven, I instantly think it's not an important game. At school you may have had various configurations in the playground at lunchtime, but the honour always was to make 'the first eleven'. Okay, there are increasing numbers of subs allowed now, and it can get very tactical, but the maximum number of players you are allowed on the field is still the perfect eleven.

The ex-England manager Bobby Robson, from Stanley in County Durham, once said: 'If six of yours can play better than six of theirs, then you have a decent chance of winning.' (Based on 11-a-side). Seven, and your chances are improved. Eight, and it's a forgone conclusion. Nine, and it's a case of try to keep count of the goals. Ten, and the other team might as well not bother turning up – it's hardly a match. So, we should stick to eleven players, just to ensure that (Sir) Bobby's slide rule to football success carries on working.

Jimmy Greaves, footballer, playing for the
Chelsea Cricket Eleven, summer 1958
(Mirrorpix)

JW: But a lot of other things have changed over time: how players train; certain laws; tactics and systems; the rise of managers and coaches. The offside law was revised way back in the 1920s to make the game more entertaining,

to get more goals. Even as TV has become much more demanding today and insisting on more entertainment for the armchair masses, nothing has shifted the game from 11-a-side. So, it must work. No one seriously argues that because today's players are so much fitter and faster and do twice as much running as those baggy-shorted men of yesteryear, that we need fewer players on the pitch to make it exciting.

SRC: This means that once upon a time in football history the game was like an open book – anything could happen, anyone could play and kick a ball. Then gradually, in the name of Empire and around the factories up north and elysian green fields beneath Harrow On The Hill – we get this national agreement on the number of players, on a common pitch size, on laws being introduced. It all goes mainstream.

JW: In 1888 local merchants and businessmen got twelve clubs to step up from the north and the midlands to form this new union of clubs, the Football League. Basically this was so that they could get the timing of fixtures set in stone and publicised for the coming season. It was a sign of the new modern age of clock-time, of paying fans, and of an emerging national press. Football supporters who paid for entry for matches now needed to know exactly where and when these would take place. Regular Saturday afternoon kick-offs meant that working men could get home from work, eat and get washed, and then walk or cycle to the match. The railway network meant fans could even get to some away matches. But it wasn't so easy to convince clubs to join the new league because no-one could guarantee it would be successful.

And it did have its early teething problems. Players didn't always turn up to matches on time, so the pre-selected eleven sometimes didn't start. League officials also squabbled over details about exactly how clubs should be ranked at the season's end, even *after* the league had been launched. It was a chaotic beginning, but still rather more ordered and better organised than what had gone before.

SRC: Football, with a capital F, now had something to protect. I can see this was its first real leap in the dark. Yet once various leagues were launched and new clubs from all over joined up, football quickly became part of the national psyche.

Spurs manager Bill Nicholson and his players, following their victory over Leicester City in the FA Cup Final, clinching an historic double, 1960-61
(Mirrorpix)

League football has only seriously been interrupted twice, both times by war. What a thought: that only world wars could stop football, the sport which shaped the national sporting calendar for British people.

JW: Pretty much all the early senior professional football clubs in England and Wales were named after real places, so reading about or hearing the weekend results every winter Saturday somehow confirmed our national well-being. Football effectively became the sporting map of Britain. We even launched trawlers to go fishing, and then to war, named after football clubs. The HMS Notts County was requisitioned by the Admiralty in 1939 and was sunk by German U-boats in March 1942. The Notts County club lives on, of course though, for obvious reasons, its fans never liked talking about it 'going down' or 'sinking to the bottom' of the league table.

SRC: For a long time we believed we were in charge of the world game having bossed the seven seas with British sea power. But the game honed in the UK had already been exported. The cat was out of the bag.

In 1953 the Hungarians showed up and said: 'Okay, give us your very best eleven. We'll show you how a *real* team do it.' The Magyars had been playing a very different kind of football to us, in which any man could do a 'drag-back' or fill in at any of the ten outfield positions given his all-round gifts. Hungary was the number one team in the world at the time when they came to hallowed Wembley, where the confident home nation had never been beaten by foreign opposition. They destroyed England, 6-3. This was supposed to be our sacred turf at the heart of England, a land which saw off every threat of invasion. This defeat truly upset the English apple-cart.

JW: And it got worse: the next year England went out to Budapest, planning to avenge this defeat, only to get thrashed again, this time 7 -1. The Scots also played this Hungary team home and away and lost both times. Communism triumphed – at football. It was the moment when the British game might have been jolted out of its complacency. Our island-nation was slowly awaking from the assumption that we would always be able to teach the rest of the world how to play football.

But this view was hard to shake, even though our clubs struggled in the new European tournaments. Our domestic competitions seemed like they had it all – and in a sense they did. In the fifties and sixties, small town clubs in England could still collect together the best eleven players they could muster and win titles and play in cup finals. Look at the success in the early 1960s of one of the founders of the Football League, modest Lancashire Burnley, reputedly the first club in the world to build a training ground rather than train in their home stadium. Burnley were Football League champions in 1960. Back then, wages were limited, contracts binding, and good players could be retained by the smaller clubs. Transfers and contracts were controlled by chairmen, not by players and agents. An occasional player escaped abroad, but very few British footballers wanted a move to improve their 'lifestyle.'

SRC: There's something quite heroic and more inclusive yelling at me from those photographs that mark this period, when austerity and the post-war grey began to show glimpses of colour as the instamatic camera, became more available.

There's this rather humble way that teams of the day come across as 'we are all in it together'. And yet, these photos say very little about the individual journeys and

West Ham United team, 1964, photographed at home, complete with unswept terraces
(Mirrorpix)

hardships that players might have endured to make the team at that moment.

Pictures of Chelsea FC from that period carry a very personal message for me. When I was young, my family gave a temporary home every summer to various kids from London who didn't have much in life or much to say for themselves. But they did seem to light up at the mention of Chelsea FC and Stamford Bridge. So, I started to think that there was something very special about that blue Chelsea strip, and that beneath the Stamford Bridge flowed some very good water which could offer up fantastic football teams, a match for anyone.

JW: Because of these quirks in our past, acquaintances made, or a football ground we were taken to in our youth, it is quite easy to develop ties with another club, links that may be difficult to explain but that we just can't shake off.

SRC: Definitely my story. I am made in Watford, yet Chelsea – because of my London visitors' connection – is also part of my football DNA. Burnley and 1961 double-winning Spurs were the best two teams in the land when I was born, so I also have an elevated, retrospective respect for them.

A Hungarian I know has a Liverpool FC tattoo on her

With A Splash Of Frenchman' - **Leeds United, 1992**
(SRC)

back, all because in the sixties her Hungarian dad started looking to England (football and the Beatles) and its fab teams after his own Magical Magyars (one defeat in six years) got broken up in 1956. Bill Shankly was a native socialist who would have understood the importance of the Hungarian uprising.

JW: The public thirst for the British game in the 1950s was married to that post-war feeling of recovery – of austerity's days being numbered. The nation stepped forward together through its clamour for football, even though we all followed our different clubs. I thought

the *Charles Buchan Football Monthly* and then *Kenneth Wolstenholme's* Christmas annuals of the 1960s reflected a new sporting outlook: a message that we needed no more than *this* team of eleven keen, fit young men to succeed.

So far, these elevens had largely been made up of home-grown players. A handful – John Charles, Jimmy Greaves, Gerry Baker, Denis Law among them – went abroad to earn some decent money. But few British stars stayed away for very long and very few foreign players ever came to play in Britain. It was still a remarkably insular British game – each to their own.

The Hungary football team visit the Pathé News Studio in London to
watch the film of their 6-3 demolition of England at Wembley Stadium,
the previous day, November 1953
(Mirrorpix)

SRC: But we had really good players in Britain in the sixties. The Scots were very strong and, fabulously – they are still heralded today – the West Ham United academy provided the backbone of the England World Cup winning team of '66. This vision of top quality home-grown talent is confirmed by the picture on the previous page of the club's players lined up on the Upton Park terraces. No one had even bothered to clean 'the studio' and the saintly Bobby Moore is made to stand on an empty crisp packet. Donning shorter shorts than ever before, these players are surely a symbol of the youthful bravado and modernism of the time – showing more athletic flesh – not hiding behind anything.

JW: So, what do you think finally changed our ideas about our best eleven players being British, all playing for British clubs? How did we learn to do things differently?

SRC: Bobby Robson's Ipswich had imported stars – proven Dutch players – but I believe the punt taken on the introduction of an unknown Eric Cantona broke the English mould. Now the idea grew that clubs might tweak their team with the introduction of an *Eric* from abroad – a small risk taken and yet it could just work out.

Leeds United, who signed Cantona, had a core of top British players: Gary Speed, Gordon Strachan, David Batty. It transpired – sheer genius on the manager's part – that all

they needed to do was add into their mix a Gallic genius (at odds with his own country) and this would get them across the winning-line. Okay, he only played 15 league games for Leeds in the run-in of the 1991-1992 season, but *CAN-TO-NA* added that extra *je ne sais quoi* at a crucial time. He had an even bigger effect at Manchester United when he moved there.

JW: Certainly, foreign talent has reached a near saturation level in the Premier League today (more like a World League, only one-third British players). This need to import talent may be a lesson we can indirectly trace back to those hammerings in the 1950s, by Ferenc Puskas and his Hungarian team-mates.

SRC: All I can say is that my dad came home from Wembley in 1953 after *his* England had been thrashed by Hungary and, not normally a drinker, he knocked back a large gin & tonic before retiring straight to bed. From that time on he never took any foreign player or foreign team for granted. If his beloved Watford FC were drawn against some unknown (to him) Bulgarian side, say in the UEFA Cup, then that loss to Hungary always had him suspecting that we would fall short as a club and as a football nation. Talent was also *out there*.

FA Cup Final line-up, cartoon, 1967
(Mirrorpix)

JW: We could be discussing an early Brexit and quotas for foreigners here. But I think we agree that competition against the very best and the inward flow of migrant talent to Britain has enriched the British club game, transforming our football ideas and our teams of home-grown 11-a-sides, much for the better.

Has it improved the national team? Debatable.

CHAPTER 3

Manager Needed

'Herbert Chapman Statue' - Arsenal, 2014
(SRC)

SRC: So, we eventually learned that eleven home-grown players may not, in and of themselves, be enough to build great football sides. Or even good ones.

But there's another actor in all this. He was never part of the first eleven (as if it was ever all down to them). We also developed in Britain the cult of the manager, a man who is often held up today as almost equal to the input of the entire team.

JW: Opinions about managers dominate football talk today, but most early football clubs in Britain got by without what we would recognise now as a football manager. They had a secretary, someone who looked after the players (and the general running of the club) during the week, and a trainer – a fitness man – who made sure that the players were fit and ready to play. But it was the board, the directors, who usually picked the team at most clubs. And club directors did most of the scouting and made decisions on who to sign and how much to pay. The football manager only really became widely recognised in Britain from the mid-1950s. An exception was the Yorkshireman Herbert Chapman, who back in the 1920s and 1930s became *the* first great football Svengali in Britain. He was a true visionary, a man way ahead of his time.

SRC: His statue outside the Emirates is impressive. But then Chapman, the son of a coal-miner, was a very remarkable man. He took an unfashionable northern club Huddersfield Town and managed them out of mediocrity to *three* consecutive league titles – champions of all England.

JW: And then, blow the house down, he went south to sophisticated Arsenal and did the same with them. In fact, he brought the very first league championship to the south. Yes, it took until 1931, forty-three years after the Football League had been formed, for the south of England to catch up with the industrial north. What kept them? Southern clubs not joining the early Football

'Manager Up In The Air - Sean Dyche' - Burnley, 2014
(SRC)

Brian Clough then a player for Sunderland FC,
at home with his record collection, January 1964
(Mirrorpix)

League was obviously a barrier. Herbert Chapman was certainly much more than a great coach: he took complete charge of the football and marketing side at Arsenal, unusual for its day *(I wonder if Arsene will get a statue, too?).*

Chapman not only built great sides at two very different clubs, north and south, but he understood tactics, negotiated smart deals, mastered man management, and promoted great teamwork. He fostered revolutionary ideas about how the game could appeal more to its supporters and he recognised, even then, the importance of the media. He wanted TV coverage, floodlights, white footballs, numbers on shirts and distinctive kits, well before these became fashionable. Arsenal's world-famous outfit of red with white sleeves was invented by Chapman, in 1933. Funnily enough, it was almost the same strip adopted in 1947 by the club in the town of his birth, Rotherham United.

SRC: Between then and the Premier League era, we have had some managerial greats. Jock Stein, Bill Nicholson,

Matt Busby, Don Revie and the incomparable Bill Shankly a man who, while manager at Carlisle United and then Grimsby Town, introduced a public-address system (he always liked to talk). He even embarrassed one of the Town eleven over the tannoy one day by talking publicly about the player's domestic strife. Shankly wanted his clubs to 'come home' to the fans. In Liverpool he could turn up, unannounced, at supporters' funerals.

JW: Football crowds were falling in the sixties, precisely because there were other options in life – other things to do – like spending more time in your house, watching TV or playing the latest Frank Sinatra disc on your Dansette record player!

SRC: In the *football coming of age in the modern period* 1960s, I guess it was an opinionated joker, Brian Clough, who best symbolised the brash, new version of the young football manager for the television age. That Sunderland team photo of Clough, a player with a pipe, says a lot! When he got seriously injured in 1962, Clough took on added responsibility by going into management. He was only 30. Soon he became a TV voice, a personality, as much as a football boss. People say they tuned in to watch the football highlights but really to hear the bone-dry Clough's opinions.

JW: The British press was becoming increasingly interested in celebrity lives beyond the football ground – the lifestyles of players and managers alike. Big names overseeing the game were almost expected to have big egos, and TV was the populist arena in which to spin them out. Alex Ferguson, another former player with a truncated career and strong views, appeared to be a one-off, but he actually came from a great line of exceptional and knowledgeable Scottish football managers.

SRC: But where are the great English football managers now?

JW: In the 1960s, home-grown successful British managers were tough cookies, men who could bring all the necessary ingredients together to forge a winning team. At that time Scottish and north east mining communities appeared to be like a sporting blast furnace for producing the ideal managerial mould. Some committed Scottish bosses – like the genius Jock Stein – even died on the job.

Brian Clough, manager at 31 years of age, with his Derby County team, October 1967
(Mirrorpix)

The last *English* manager to win the league title was Howard Wilkinson, at Leeds United, and that was even before the Premier League was formed. Perhaps we do have a thing here for *nearly* men. Sir Bobby Robson was a partial exception but even he was more noted for his management career abroad. He became a national treasure, of course, but mainly perhaps for being an honourable man more than a really great manager.

Most people would say today that someone like Sean Dyche has done a very decent job as a top level English football manager. But no-one would say he's a Bobby Robson, never mind a Clough, a Bill Shankly or a Fergie.

SRC: It's clear that at the very top level the impact of a great manager can make the difference. In the late-nineties Arsene Wenger changed both Arsenal and the entire English game. But lower down the ladder? Do smaller clubs need managers at all?

JW: Most of those successful guys in the second, third and fourth tiers tend to be grounded and humble – just an extension of the team really. Most of the old northern players who went on to become good managers were saved from manual jobs, in the pits and factories, saved by a better life in football. So, these are not people who are necessarily sent by God; they're shift managers who just have to work with what they've got and try to make a silk purse out of not very much.

Before the Premier League came along, most top players only really respected other men who had played the game and had a decent career: the 'one-of-us' hand me downs. These days, other routes have opened up –

Players Alex Ferguson and Bert Paton exercising
for Dunfermline Athletic, March 1966
(Mirrorpix)

Jock Stein, manager of Scotland, stumbles and collapses, watched by
assistant manager Alex Ferguson at the end of Wales V Scotland
match at Ninian Park in Cardiff, 1985
(Mirrorpix)

in various forms of coaching and management – as elite football has become more analytical, more reliant on research and on devising new 'scientific' systems of play. It's a brainier business today. Now there is more chance that you can make players believe in you if you can show them that you have seen the data, understand the game, and can control a group of anxious, ambitious egos. You no longer have to have served in the trenches to be trusted in the dressing room.

SRC: And yet, all managers in the end (like politicians) suffer the same fate – except maybe for Arsene Wenger and Sir Alex Ferguson. It drives people like me to distraction that the tenure of managers today seems to get shorter and shorter, and still we talk more and more about replacing them. 'Six defeats in a row and you're sacked' has become an accepted algorithm.

Sometimes, when the tabloids and radio talk-shows bore on and on about sacking a manager and the public gets sucked into the debate, I wish we could just get rid of managers entirely. Let teams run themselves and prove their worth or collapse trying.

JW: Think on. Without Graham Taylor, your very own club Watford FC would have been very average in the 1980s. He changed the club from top to bottom – or bottom to top. I don't think we would want to pass up the opportunity of having really special football managers moving amongst our men. I don't even think that we could get by easily without a group of more standard managers – certainly the board can't do it, the fans can't do it, and the players need a guide, and someone to blame when things go wrong.

Like it or not, managers ARE needed.

CHAPTER 4

Who Owns The Club?

JW: So, it's heaven's will that:

1. *Good managers can build a great team*
2. *They don't have to be British (these days)*
3. *They CAN turn a struggling club around – if they are a Graham Taylor.*

But there is a group of people above them: financiers, actors and wheeler-dealers, some genuinely capable people, who we can't ignore. These are the men behind the scenes who run and own football clubs – or think they do.

SRC: I like the story of a local man, Jack Walker, buying a very traditional football club in Blackburn Rovers in the 1990s, arriving in a standard saloon with his mates outside Ewood Park, rolling up his sleeves and saying: 'Well, I can bring something to this party. I've got some money, I know what to do.' Jack's the local maverick figure: 'Job to do, better be getting on with it' mentality. Walker's business background was steel, but he could have been a (rich) plumber one supposes. He never took his eye off the ball and then when his chance came along…

JW: A rover's return. But what exactly do owners bring to the party? Is it payback time? Once upon a time people like you and I might have believed in a local guy who put his money and time into the club and we probably would have presumed he was doing a good job for the local community. But things have changed. Whilst managers could only get a job in a club if they had some sort of football pedigree, owners just needed hard cash, some business acumen, possibly some bluster. Two out of three would usually do it.

SRC: In the 1960s, when football fans were beginning to choose their own lifestyles and preferences, doubts about owners were already stirring: 'Hold on – my father and his father watched this club. Don't mess it up.' And by the 2000s this view was keener still: 'You can't waltz in now and start talking about owning our club, just because you have money'.

People have started cultivating, collecting and valuing the history of their football clubs – almost any club in the land – and are even keeping an eye on other clubs that are not their own. They get indignant over the mistreatment of fellow supporters. Because of generations of support handed down, they think themselves to be, somehow, the real custodians of their clubs, seeing the whole football landscape as some kind of elaborate family history puzzle.

JW: That's the romantic version. But trying telling that to the people – whatever you might say about them – who have legally bought the club with real money and have done all the paperwork to say it's *theirs*.

SRC: Jack Walker back in 1991, flush with £360 million from selling his Walkersteel company, is definitely different from the owners who followed him later in the Premier League era. Assem Allam, the British-Egyptian owner of a Rolls-Royce and Hull City FC, in his public statements, makes his motives *sound* like Jack Walker's: an obligation to pay back the region for his own success. But whilst Blackburn-born Jack wanted his Rovers to return to being the successful club of his youth, Assem took over Hull City in 2010 and wanted change for the future. Naively perhaps, he had visions of furry tigers selling well in the Far East and making his club more marketable worldwide. Jack Walker's ambitions were much more local.

Sucked along in the global Premier League boom (and Hull City had got there for the first time) AA thought little of trying to switch the club's name – overturning 100

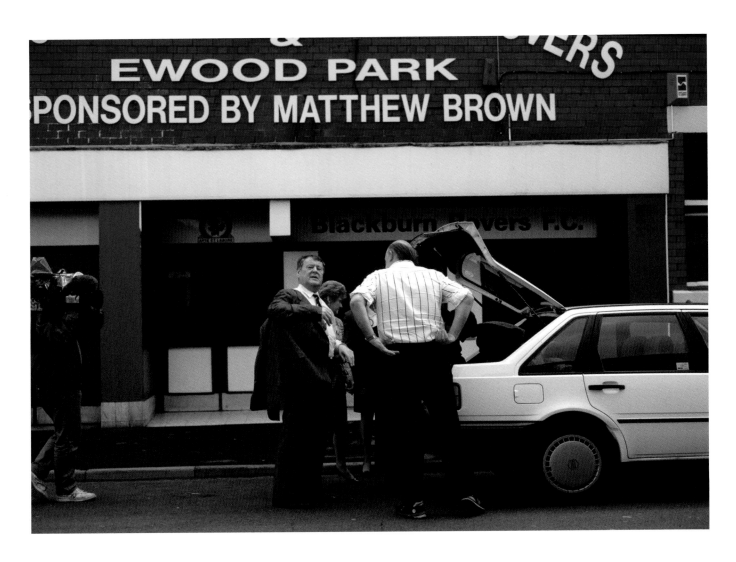

'The Arrival Of Jack Walker' - **Blackburn Rovers, 1992**
(SRC)

years of tradition – all part of a day or two in the office considering the marketing and modernisation of Hull City. *The fans turned against him.* Roared against him in fact. At most clubs, if not at Rovers and Hull City, what the fans collectively pay at the turnstile, on pre-match ticket sales and in buying extras like shirts and merchandise, still exceeds the cash put in or loaned by the 'owner'.

JW: A postmodern, global football tale. In the past, football clubs introduced local business people into some very powerful and influential networks. Imagine, too, the income you might conjure directly from football if you

were, say, a lawyer, a brewer, a pie-maker or a builder. Over time, football fans pretty much forgot who owned their clubs. Owners in the 1980s wanted no public profile. People on the board were generally a bit boring, aside from Watford's Elton John, a glitzy exception.

The reality is that most football clubs lost money – most still do. Keeping a local club alive in hard times was what supporters relied on local club owners and directors to manage. Football clubs have gone bust, of course, but few of them disappear.

Directors rolled up to the club AGM every year, listened to a few disgruntled voices, and then set about the new

'The Chairman And His Prize' - Hull City, 2013
(SRC)

season running it much as before. But probably nothing like the way they ran their own businesses. Football was a weekend hobby, with a few more cigars thrown in and they faced little opposition. The fanzine culture of the 1980s did, however, stir things up a little. Fans have had to learn much more since about football business.

SRC: Some clubs, like Millwall for example, seem to feel like that can never really be 'owned' at all because they're just such a spiky club. If the Lord Himself came down to walk through those formidable gates to reorganise the embattled Den, Millwall fans would probably say: 'Sorry guv'nor, hands off. This is *our* club.' Millwall fans – and there are one or two other examples, West Ham United, for one – seem bent on 'owning' their club in the sort of muscular way that just isn't in the character of many other football places.

JW: Yes, West Ham supporters have certainly been narked by owners who levered the club out of their loved home and then promised the moon. Take another case, well-meaning Vincent Tan at Cardiff City. Here is an owner with his own revolutionary ideas: change the club's historic colours from blue to red to make Cardiff City the national club of Wales. Science had also told him that red was the proven colour of winners. Which is actually not so crazy because the great physicist Stephen Hawking also argued that science proved that playing in red and in a 4-3-3 formation held the best prospect for football success. Hawking also devised a formula for taking penalty kicks: high shots by bald, fair haired players were the best bet. Who knew?

Vincent Tan, however, failed miserably to win Cardiff supporters over and, science or no science, Bluebirds fans soon kicked his revolutionary crystal ball clean over the popular stand.

'Entrance To The Old Den' - Millwall, 1991
(SRC)

SRC: The Glazers bought Manchester United in 2005 and also borrowed money against the football business to clinch the deal. United had some success but also lost hundreds of millions of pounds in interest charges and dividends to the owners and their family.

Some United radicals decided to go back to their roots with a new club, FC United of Manchester, because they were enraged by the goings on at Old Trafford. They felt manipulated by owners from thousands of miles away. FC United's mantra is: 'We are the club the club is us. We are not for profit. We own defeat, we own failure. We can't walk away.' Success for FC United is making ends meet and having a good time while raising a standard. FC United aims to maintain a set of values which they believed had gone AWOL at corporatised Manchester United. The red heart is their flag, not the dollar sign.

JW: Even FCUM have had their recent upheavals. We live in new times. For most of the history of the English game, making money from football was really not that easy, but today foreign investors are falling over each other to milk what looks like a Premier League cash cow.

Spending money in English football also buys you soft power: the Chinese, the people from Qatar, the Manchester Sheiks, Roman Abramovich at Chelsea. Who's next? Who is richer still? These are the kind of people – and governments – who have so much money they can get bored by their own vast wealth. What to do with all that cash? What looks interesting and has influence? What are people talking about? Where can I meet other super-

powerful people, like me? The Premier League ticks a lot of these boxes. It's become a playpen for the global uber rich.

SRC: It's a kind of bling checklist, isn't it? Buy a massive yacht! Tick. Buy *one, two, three, four, five, six*, at least *seven* houses in the most magnificent locations in the world. Tick. Buy my partner whatever he, or she, wants. Tick. Give away a few of your global businesses for the kids to play with. Tick. And then people start to ask you: 'Why haven't you bought a football club?' This new set of uber-rich global club owners may not always be in football for the good of the game.

JW: But when a club is in real trouble, or just ambitious for change, even die-hard fans can sometimes close their eyes and cross their fingers. Supporters' groups, which may have spent years wrestling the club back from reckless owners or from possible extinction, can sometimes give in to the easier path of a rich benefactor. And so, the crazy cycle goes on. In the end – and even at the lower levels of the game – more money will always be needed. Expectations become inflated.

'Simple Pure Love Affair' - FC United, 2015
(SRC)

SRC: It's also true that, faced with a vacuum – standing still, or a potential investor who pulls out – there might even be a reluctant acceptance of the return of the old maligned board: to men who had a few bob between them, didn't give up, but rather watched from the wings or from behind the curtains as it all went pear-shaped. Then, like the *Thunderbirds*, they are back in for the unlikely

'The Chairman's Dream Of Too Much On His Plate' - Carlisle United, 1993
(SRC)

rescue. It happened at my own local club, Carlisle United. Owners often want their cake – and other people's cake as well – and want to scoff the lot.

JW: There are still some good people around, owners from home and abroad, people who want the very best for their clubs and for the fans who support them. Like Steve Gibson at Middlesbrough, who has pumped money in and stuck by his hometown club. And fans have also sensibly stepped in – heroically in some cases – to rescue some smaller clubs that may have flown too close to the sun or been duped by imposters.

SRC: In fact, the more I think about it, it's patently clear what people like Jack Walker at Blackburn Rovers were all about. As the owner of local businesses employing half the town, Jack saved up everyone else's money and then gave a good deal of it back – he reinvested it in the local football club. And because this took bigger clubs by surprise, he even carried his unfashionable town to the Premier League title in 1995.

JW: More than that, he did all of this on the site of Ewood Park, where almost the entire Rovers story had been played out since the club helped found the Football League back in 1888. He expanded and modernised the stadium, of course, but it is still surrounded by those familiar neighbourhood streets, Victorian houses where the club's earliest players and their families once lived.

SRC: 'The house that the locally-raised Jack built' raises another dynamic – if you happen to come from afar to buy an English football club in an age when television is king, why do you need to keep it in the same place it has always been? Why does Ewood Park, or Deepdale, or 'home' matter at all in these increasingly placeless times? There was that string of adverts, which talked about moving Arsenal to the Peak District in Derbyshire where there was a bit more space for development. Not so far off someone else's truth.

Arsenal, when they moved from Highbury to not far away, at least tried to preserve the memory and integrity of their hemmed-in, once great ground. They turned their glorious turf into a park and some of the stands became (expensive) homes. People could still 'worship' there and walk the dog. It should always be the responsibility of the owner or caretaker in selling off any football ground to make sure it becomes a place of pilgrimage. Take Roker Park: over the course of its lifetime it has hosted literally millions of people having the time of their lives through football. How can it possibly be that when time was finally called on this historic venue they simply knocked it down, flattened it; abused its memory? They sold it off for a few medium quality houses. The developers' only concession was to label roads within the new estate, Turnstile Mews, Midfield Drive, Promotion Close, etc. This is quite pathetic. Would one have knocked down a church with so little care? Who is this supposed to benefit? There were, and are still, loads of scruffy bits of land just a stone's throw away from the old Roker Park which could have been built on. It's as if someone - a force from within even - wants to do down the very things we most hold dear. It feel like a local form of self-harm but on a national scale, because there are numerous equivalents of Roker Park. Let's hope the same fate does not await historic Goodison Park. These are sacred places, where we have most felt at home.

JW: And pity the fans of those league clubs today that cannot be sure of a home at all. In February 2019 Coventry City were given just two months by the Football League to find a stadium in which they could play their home fixtures in 2019/20. City's hedge fund proprietors had no agreement in place with the Ricoh Stadium owners Wasps, a Premiership Rugby club. Here was a great football club, potentially homeless in 2019. How did we get here?'

CHAPTER 5

Playing At Home

'Big Open Discussion' - Barnsley, 2014
(SRC)

SRC: The idea of home for me, is of an immovable object: it's a material thing of course, but it is also an identity and a sense of place. Home is where most of us want to be at Xmas - with our families - and home in a football sense is just an extension of this. A site where your forefathers and mothers also trod. It has a history. It's yours to decorate.

JW: Home has a very special meaning in football, of course: we speak a lot about 'playing at home' and being 'drawn at home' and 'home advantage.' It certainly seems to make a major difference to results. The statistics say that, on average, home teams win more than half their games whilst away teams only win one quarter. That's quite a split. Referees can be swayed by a home crowd. And clubs can have problems switching homes - check out the recent West Ham situation. How is it that a stadium and its fans can mean so much?

SRC: It doesn't add up. Even if you play a match at home with no fans (behind closed doors) it's still an advantage.

Maybe the ghosts of home supporters are cheering you on?

Most football fans have a central message. No matter how shambolic you might think our ground is, we really LOVE this place. Most football grounds were not set up to be especially beautiful palaces, but they were always a safe space for locals. A spiritual place. A place of pilgrimage. An altar, of sorts.

We won't go on here about football as a substitute for religion, but a stadium *is* a kind of sacred gathering ground, a destination, an Oz at the end of the rainbow. Just as Glastonbury has come to signify much more than an ancient religious centre, a football ground is active and earthquakes of the human spirit regularly happen there.

JW: 'Earthquakes of the human spirit' is a wonderful phrase. The home football ground is not just about bricks and concrete, that's clear. It is much more about what the stadium *means* to local people: a beautifully painted wall, or some familiar and friendly girders can carry all kinds of messages and comfort, missed by most of us. But it is also about how aspects of that meaning can make it an oppressive and threatening place for visitors, the enemy. Being an away fan is enjoyable - the trip and all that invasive singing and chanting - but it's also a kind of intrusion. Sometimes, you can feel like an unwelcome and a very unappreciated guest in the away end. And each football club has its own message for visitors, encoded in its stadium. There is a kind of siege mentality thing which goes on around 'our' home patch. Only when something huge that affects us all occurs - like a Hillsborough, for example - can football fans easily pull together and share a truly collective identity and the associated pain.

SRC: Hillsborough was obviously a key moment, a time when we had to reflect on what we valued about our

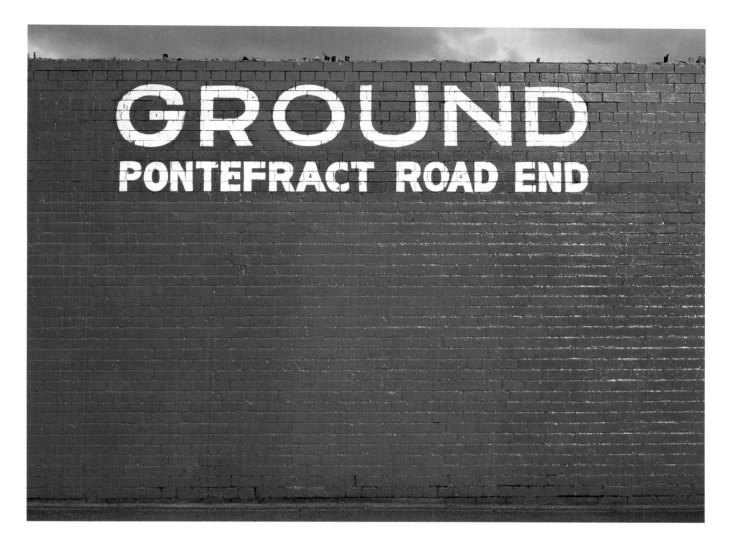

'Blood Red Road End' - Barnsley, 1993
(SRC)

existing homes and what urgently needed to change. Some of those favourite nooks and crannies, which defined our homes – which made them ours – would now have to go. Could we hold on to the soul of our football grounds?

JW: We could all see, I think, that Lord Justice Taylor's pronouncements in 1990 after Hillsborough were going to produce a new football stadium experience; a much bigger shift than the impact of player transfers, or even the new TV deals. They were going to change our very homes. Some of us might have complained in the past about poor facilities, terrible toilets or even difficulties in seeing the match in some grounds. We may have wanted to wash our hands of some of the old eyesores, but we were still pretty clear-eyed about keeping all existing Football League clubs and defending their homes. Non-fans must have wondered why.

SRC: What distinguishes this country is that there are SO MANY clubs and identities cheek by jowl with the next. We value them all as part of the national football story. Germans and Scandinavians and others look on in amazement (and envy) at this. A dozen

*'Green And Pleasant
Football Land'*, 2019

By Stuart Roy Clarke
& Stuart Beveridge ©

UNST
BALTASOUND
HARRISON
PARK

WHALSAY

THURSO
THE VIKINGS

DURNESS

HALKIRK UNITED
RECREATION PARK
THE ANGLERS

WICK ACADEMY
THE SCORRIES
HARMSWORTH
PARK
GOLSPIE
SUTHERLAND
KING GEORGE
V PARK
BALINTORE
SEABOARD
PARK

INVERNESS
FIVEPENNY

CARLOWAY
CHNOC A'
CHOILICH
STORNOWAY
ATHLETIC
STORNOWAY
UNITED
BACK

LOCHBROOM
THE CATTACHS
DUDGEON PARKS RANGERS
BRORA
RANGERS
ALNESS
UNITED
DALMORE PARK
ROSS COUNTY
THE STAGGIES
VICTORIA
PARK
CLACHNACUDDIN
INVERNESS CITY GRANT STREET
PARK
NORTHERN MEETING PARK
FORRES MECHANICS
MOSSET PARK
THE CAN CANS

LOSSIEMOUTH
THE COASTERS
GRANT PARK

FRASERBURGH
THE BROCH
BELLSLEA PARK

PETERHEAD
BALMOOR
THE BLUE TOON
TURRIFF UNITED
THE HAUGHS
FORMARTINE UNITED
NORTH LODGE PARK

BENBECULA

STAFFIN
PORTREE

KYLEAKIN
KYLE OF
LOCHALSH

"SUPER CALEY GO
BALLISTIC CELTIC
ARE ATROCIOUS"

INVERNESS
CALEDONIAN
THISTLE
CALEDONIAN
STADIUM

NAIRN
COUNTY
STATION
PARK

BUCKIE THISTLE
THE JAGS
VICTORIA PARK

KEITH
KYNOCH PARK
THE MAROONS

ROTHES
MACKESSACK PARK
PRINCESS
DEVERONVALE

ELGIN CITY
BOROUGH
BRIGGS
DUFFTOWN
THE TOONSERS

HUNTLY
CHRISTIE PARK
BLACK AND GOLDS

COVE RANGERS
HIGHLAND
DYNAMITE
ALLAN PARK

FORT
WILLIAM

CLAGGAN
PARK

PLOCKTON

STRATHSPEY
THISTLE

SEAFIELD PARK

INVERURIE LOCO WORKS
THE LOCIES HARLAW PARK
CROMBIE PARK
CULTER

ABERDEEN
PITTODRIE
THE DONS

MONTROSE
LINKS PARK

BLANEFIELD
THISTLE

VALE OF ATHOLL
"COME AWAY THE VALE"

THE HEDGEMEN
BRECHIN CITY
GLEBE PARK

SUNNYBANK
HEATHRYFOLD PARK
BANKS O' DEE
SPAIN PARK

THE GABLE
ENDIES

OBAN SAINTS
GLENCRUITTEN PARK

BLAIRGOWRIE JUNIOR
THE BERRYPICKERS
DAVIE PARK
DUNBLANE
THISTLE

FORFAR ATHLETIC
THE LOONS
STATION PARK

ARBROATH
GAYFIELD
PARK
THE RED
LICHTIES

GREENOCK
MORTON
CAPPIELOW
PARK

ST. JOHNSTONE
McDIARMID
PARK

DUNDEE
DENS PARK

DUNDEE UNITED
TANNADICE PARK
THE TERRORS

CLYDEBANK
THE BANKIES

THE PRIDE
OF CLYDE

CALLANDER SEVEN ACRES PARK
THISTLE THE TANGERINES
LETHAM

EAST FIFE
BAYVIEW
STADIUM

HOLM PARK

GLASGOW CITY
PETERSHILL PARK

PARTICK
THISTLE
THE JAGS

RAITH
ROVERS
STARK'S
PARK

CARRADALE

LOCHGILPHEAD
RED STAR

RANGERS
IBROX
GERS

STIRLING
ALBION
FORTHBANK
STADIUM

STENHOUSEMUIR
OCHILVIEW PARK

DUNFERMLINE
ATHLETIC
EAST END PARK
THE PARS

BURNTISLAND
SHIPYARD

QUEEN'S
PARK
HAMPDEN
PARK

CELTIC
THE BHOYS
CELTIC PARK

CAMELON JUNIORS
THE MARINERS
CARMUIRS PARK

FALKIRK
THE BAIRNS

ALBION
ROVERS
CLIFTONHILL

AIRDRIEONIANS
NEW BROOMFIELD
DIAMONDS

HIBERNIAN
HIBEES
EASTER
ROAD

KILMARNOCK
RUGBY PARK

MOTHERWELL
THE STEELMEN
FIR PARK

AUCHINLECK
TALBOT
BEECHWOOD
PARK

HAMILTON
ACADEMICAL
NEW DOUGLAS
PARK

LIVINGSTON
ALMONDVALE

HEART OF MIDLOTHIAN
HEARTS HEARTS
GLORIOUS
HEARTS
TYNECASTLE

BERWICK
RANGERS
SHIELFIELD
PARK

GIRVAN
THE SEASIDERS
HAMILTON PARK

GLENBUCK
CHERRYPICKERS
BURNSIDE

CUMNOCK
JUNIORS

AYR UNITED
SOMERSET PARK

TOWNHEAD
PARK

GLENAFTON
ATHLETIC
THE LIONS

GRETNA
RAYDALE PARK

ALNWICK
THE COLLIERS

ASHINGTON
WOODHORN LANE

THE HONEST MEN

ANNAN
ATHLETIC
GALABANK

THE ANVILS

MORPETH
TOWN
BEDLINGTON TERRIERS
DOCTOR PIT WELFARE PARK
NORTH SHIELDS THE MORGUE

STRANRAER
STAIR PARK

QUEEN OF
THE SOUTH
PALMERSTON PARK
DOONHAMERS

CARLISLE
SHEEPMOUNT

CARLISLE
UNITED
BRUNTON PARK

NEWCASTLE UNITED
ST JAMES PARK
"TOON ARMY TOON ARMY"

LINFIELD
THE BLUES
WINDSOR
PARK

CRUSADERS
SEAVIEW
THE HATCHETMEN

SKY BLUES
BALLYMENA
UNITED
GLENAVON
MOURNEVIEW PARK
THE BRIDESMAIDS

CLIFTONVILLE
SOLITUDE
THE REDS

LISBURN
DISTILLERY
THE WHITES
NEW GROSVENOR
STADIUM

COLERAINE
BANNSIDERS
THE SHOWGROUNDS

DERRY CITY
BRANDYWELL
STADIUM
CANDYSTRIPES

GLENTORAN
THE COCK N HENS
THE OVAL

NEWRY CITY
THE TOWN
SHOWGROUNDS

WORKINGTON
BOROUGH PARK

BARROW
HOLKER STREET
BLUE BIRDS

BRAITHWAITE

AMBLESIDE
UNITED

ULLSWATER

SUNDERLAND
STADIUM OF LIGHT
BLACK CATS
SUNDERLAND RCA
MEADOW PARK

MORECAMBE
THE SHRIMPS
GLOBE
ARENA

WINDERMERE

CONISTON

KENDAL
TOWN
PARKSIDE

SPENNYMOOR TOWN

BISHOP AUCKLAND
THE TWO BLUES
HERITAGE PARK

HARTLEPOOL
UNITED
MONKEY
HANGERS
VICTORIA PARK

KIRKBY STEPHEN

THE DOLLY BLUES
LANCASTER CITY
GIANT AXE

BLACKPOOL
ROVERS

BLACKBURN

ACCRINGTON
STANLEY

MIDDLESBROUGH
BORO
RIVERSIDE

BILLINGHAM
SYNTHONIA

THE SHELLS
SHILDON

DARLINGTON

THE SEADOGS
SCARBOROUGH

ST. GEORGES
GLENEARTNEY? ROAD

'Maine Road Was Where It Was At' - Manchester City, 2011
(SRC)

Norwegians arrive at Grimsby Town's Blundell Park from across the North Sea (not in Viking boats, I might add) and they are soon taking group selfies against the plain old terraced houses neighbouring the ground.

Visitors are fascinated by all this historic detail we have around our football places. Not everything is perfectly arranged in the national football grid, of course, it's all a bit higgledy-piggledy. It's like a mad jigsaw – where is the plan? There may not have been one; football just sort of happened in this way, it took root around the nation. The locals in Cleethorpes feel honoured, of course, that visiting Norwegians want to photograph their old houses – they even sweep the front step.

I am sure stadiums – our homes – that were sited in densely peopled areas, rather than plonked like a business unit in an industrial estate, speak to us much more as fans. When Manchester City moved across the city to the Etihad in 2003 the club instinctively knew that they had to take something of the old ground, their old home, with them. The Maine Road stone is a memorial to the former place and its people. It's repositioned today outside one of the posh entrances at the Etihad and is possibly the single-most photographed bit of the new ground.

I must say I am cheered by the fact that the British were shown at this moment to care very deeply about its football culture.

JW: Collectively we cried at Hillsborough and the events of 1989 and collectively we responded to what Lord Justice Taylor said in his report and with some spirit of togetherness we rolled out the red carpet for the game's return, possibly to a new golden period. We prioritised it and got the thing rebuilt not quite overnight but over a few years and moreover – *with some care and with some love.*

CHAPTER 6

Fans Needed

West Ham fans queue at Upton Park, as tickets for their FA Cup match
against Fulham go on sale. February 1958
(Mirrorpix)

'Forest Crowd Up Against It' - Nottingham Forest at Aston Villa,1991
(SRC)

'Semi Final Crowd' - West Ham United at Aston Villa, 1991
(SRC)

SRC: So we've got the whole picture of football now. You forget your hands, kick a ball around, call yourself a player, form yourself into teams of eleven, get yourself managed, find somewhere to call home, with a built-in home advantage. What else do we need?

FANS, of course, ideally recruited through ties of family and of place. Or through success – people from all over Britain became Nottingham Forest fans in the late-1970s because of what Brian Clough achieved there.

Leeds United fans of a certain age also turn up today in the most unlikely of places. Or perhaps some of us become football fans because we feel an underdog club will one day have its place in the sun? Peculiarly, we do consciously seem to follow clubs just because they are a bit useless – perhaps further proof of our masochism and loyalty. We love a good loser.

But where did early fans come from?

JW: In the past, those residents who lived around football grounds were an important part of a club's target audience. We have seen that British football clubs were usually set up in reasonably affluent working-class areas, so that working men with a bit of money to spend could walk to the match after work on Saturday mornings. There was public transport for others – buses and trams – though supporters arriving on bikes could often park them in local gardens for a small consideration. Clubs often rented terraced houses around grounds to staff, which was useful for post-war players because most of them

didn't own cars.

The picture of London fans in the 1950s queueing in a quiet and orderly fashion is not even taken on a match-day. It's a daytime ticket collection for a fifth round West Ham versus Fulham FA Cup tie. At least some of these people must have taken time out from work. Bosses would probably have worked out that some of their employees will have nipped out of the depot, or office, for a couple of hours queuing off Green Street. Secret approval perhaps? This was, after all, a big deal locally – the magic of the FA Cup and a local derby to boot.

SRC: What do people say: that the British are 'good' at queuing in a way, say, the Italians are not? (Is there a World Cup for queuing? We would be clear favourites). The British also love a good conga, which is a bit of queuing with an obvious inability to dance thrown in.

This picture also reminds me of images of queues for wartime food rationing. Most of the people here would have had memories of those austere days from only a few years before. British people had learnt to bide their time: to sit out air raids calmly, to queue patiently. And, of course, to let the nice photographer take their picture.

In summary: the sort of people going to football in 1958 are the queuing sort. And they expect to have their photograph taken by the 'family' photographer.

JW: There are quite a few female faces in the front of this crowd. Some people might be surprised, but women have always watched the game, perhaps especially on these grand local occasions. Or are some of these women queuing on behalf of someone else, perhaps?

SRC: Over time, the overwhelming maleness of the game in Britain may have been taken for granted. Football can be a hive of pushing and shoving and blokes yelling. Sometimes it's assumed that the stadium is an arena where men can be men, can test you out or pin you with a look.

The man staring straight at me at Ipswich Town, at the end of an 'Old Farm derby' with Norwich City, took me a little by surprise. I'd already met some Town fans wearing weird animal heads in the bar beneath the stand before the match. Out on the street, managing the crowds and scanning for possible trouble, the police had earlier been confronted by packs of (mainly) friendly lions, tigers and bears. Then, in the stands whilst rival fans were still busy taunting each other, frustrated at the inconclusive drawn outcome and wanting a bit of 'afters', this tough-looking middle-aged guy stood out. Who in heavens had I met? I still took the photo, but it's not often that I have a 'stare off' quite like this one. Usually, I try to make sure that my football pictures are quite natural and well observed. I had also almost forgotten about the book 'Skinhead.' It had so left such an impression on me as a boy with its tales of violence and sex and football. And here it was again, a reminder on a t-shirt.

'A Skinhead At Heart' - Ipswich Town, 2015
(SRC)

JW: Chaos all around him, this supporter seems completely stilled, doesn't he, caught in the eye of the

FA Cup Semi Final match at Hillsborough
14th March 1959 - Nottingham Forest v Aston Villa
(Mirrorpix)

storm. David Bowie said it best: 'When you are a boy, other boys check you out.' Older boys too.

SRC: All this looks so different from the exceptional 1959 photograph of Nottingham Forest fans at an FA Cup semi-final at Hillsborough. These supporters so wanted their team to do it in the '(Manager Billy) Walker Way' – not Des, he came later. Forest did it, winning 1-0, but there is not much sense of the excited football carnival here.

Then, look at my pictures more than a generation later, of rival Forest and West Ham fans at another FA Cup semi-final, this time at Villa Park in 1991.

JW: That West Ham picture from 1991 could easily be from the 1950s: it's a very calm looking crowd, expectant but also transfixed by your camera. The guy with the over-grown rosette looks timeless. In between those two moments of calm, 32 years apart, we know that things had actually grown much uglier in the British game.

Hooliganism really started to take off in England in the late-1960s, and when Manchester United got relegated in 1974 some of their younger supporters started targeting Second Division clubs, which were even less prepared to cope with the coming onslaught. By now, rival fans in England were divided by steel fences. It's now the 'Psycho way' for Forest – Stuart Pearce, of course. And yet, if one took away the fences, they do look quite similar sorts of football gatherings, no? Only time – and fences – separate us.

Manchester United fans celebrate promotion back to the top flight,
at Notts County after a 2-2 draw, 1975
(Mirrorpix)

'Queue For Lancs Away Day' - **Blackpool at Burnley, 1998**
(SRC)

There is a picture here of a typical 'Red Army' trip to Notts County in 1975. A crush barrier seems to have been flattened in a celebratory melee. A solitary policeman looks on. It is an eerie signal of what lay ahead for the English game – serious crowd trouble and future stadium disasters.

SRC: I remember this period. When United fans came to town, businesses closed down and local residents boarded up their windows. For a while, hosting football in some places in Britain became like preparing for a visit from a hostile military unit.

If we compare this image from 1975 with one of my pictures from 1998 – back to queuing – things seemed to have settled down quite a bit.

JW: Things had changed, thankfully – but what about that advertising hoarding! In the 1950s, of course, for a few quid some top footballers would happily advertise fags, even as a health supplement. Many still smoked in the sixties, including in the tunnel on the way out to the pitch. But the idea, approaching the Millennium, that it was okay to depict a man protecting a giant pack of cigarettes over his own wife in front of young supporters like these seems outrageous now, and for all kinds of reasons. In the stands and on the terraces in the 1990s you could still be watching the game through a fug of cigarette smoke. Smoking at football was still expected rather than outlawed. Today we sell fags like hard drugs, under the counter and expensive,

in little brown parcels.

SRC: If we take a little of what kills us, in fact we might emerge stronger seems to be the philosophy here. After all, we all suffer for our clubs, through all four seasons and changeable weathers, and we can stumble about for decades through a trophy desert. Few clubs in football win anything much.

JW: It would be harsh, I think, to say that football sets out to make its fans suffer. Early clubs could not afford a roof to protect terrace fans, so supporters often had to cling together in rain and snow, simply to try to stay warm and dry.

But there was the view at that time that standing out, unprotected, in all weathers was somehow character-building, good for you. Even if you were busy passive smoking. Football supporting equals national service sliced up 92 times. Working men were hardy souls. Manual work was often dangerous and usually outdoors, and local football support was historically rooted in local working-class allegiances.

SRC: British football fandom has always been, at some level, about embracing suffering – proving your devotion, as you wait for the good times to come. By contrast, the USA's attempt at establishing 'soccer' never went down the fags and suffering route: they just introduced popcorn instead.

CHAPTER 7

The 'Derby' Between Us

SRC: In every pantomime, there must be a villain. Therefore, for every football club supported, there must be someone potentially to hate. Is that not true? In Britain, in media speak, we like to think of these as 'fierce' rivalries, but most British football derbies are actually quite mild.

JW: We have our problems here, local rivalries can get out of control. But in some other countries fan rivalries can mean setting out to seriously damage or even kill each other, with flares, knives and even guns being taken to the match. Argentina has recently had a spate of football fan murders.

Dundee and Dundee United in close proximity
(Courtesy of Google Maps 2018)

SRC: Raised on watching Watford FC – hardly Boca Juniors, I concede – I was encouraged to seriously dislike, to hate in fact, our local rivals Luton Town. Away from my family and football friends and now in adulthood, I can actually admit today to having a bit of a *liking* for the Hatters of Luton. After all, they helped me become the Watford supporter I am. But let's get some perspective

here: the scale of the Watford v Luton rivalry – and the geographical connections which brought these clubs together (down The M1 motorway) – are nowhere near as powerful or as meaningful as the Newcastle v Sunderland stand-offs, or the local derbies in Manchester, Sheffield, Merseyside or Glasgow. Or even the one which still divides the city of Dundee.

JW: Growing up, I remember seeing so many aerial photographs of the Dundee grounds in football annuals. The back-story was always: 'The closest football clubs in the world, less than 200 yards apart – both on the same street.' Only in Britain could two major sports stadia grow up quite like this, bumping up against each other in the same neighbourhood and in the same sport. The new football marketing men of today would almost certainly say: 'Rationalise your assets for pity's sake – share a stadium.'

SRC: Try telling British fans to share their home with a rival. They would tell you to get lost. Actually, that concept of sharing, which is intended as upsizing, really does upset fans even more perhaps than losing the local derby.

JW: There is little territorial divide for fans in Dundee, which means that people from both clubs live in each other's pockets or even share the same families. There is no escape in the 'big village' when your team loses the derby, but nor do people try to tear each other's heads off after the match.

SRC: At Dundee, the visiting players in suits, carrying their boots, walk from their home dressing-room up/down the road to their near-neighbours on derby matchdays. Some of the crowd join them. It's like a protest, but with nothing to protest about. It's fab that this can still happen.

'Hands Across The Rivalry' - Sunderland v Newcastle United, 2007
(SRC)

Are the 'best' derbies the ones where two sets of fans are going as close as they can to hatred, without crossing a line? You often hear people say about rival fans 'They absolutely hate each other', but they say it almost with admiration. Less often do you hear them say: 'How nice: they all walk down the street together'.

JW: That friendliness is surely for rugby crowds. Without disrespecting the friendly Dundee stroll, a football derby has to have some intensity of feeling: resentment, envy, arrogance, mutual intolerance, call it what you like. But I would always stop short of hatred; this isn't war.

Just look at your picture of the Wearside-Tyneside derby. Every fan from my generation who has ever travelled away will probably have a story to tell about this kind of set-up. The guy standing out in the Sunderland shirt seems to be in his own bubble, completely oblivious to the goading of the Newcastle lot. They just happen to live 14 miles apart, brought up in different sporting tribes. So, by the rules of football engagement, they're actually from entirely different worlds, especially on derby day.

SRC: They have their separate tribal colours, these rivals, but at other times these fans probably go to some of the same bars, restaurants and gigs. But in the foreground, one can still see a sporting handshake across the barricades, a couple of older guys who probably feel like they've seen it all before.

JW: Football certainly does have that 'the enemy of my enemy is a friend' thing going on. The bitter Liverpool v Manchester United regional derby only got really toxic in the 1980s, when Liverpool were doing most of the trophy winning, but Kopites claimed United got too much of the media attention for its glamour and star players.

When United finally started dominating the English game in the 1990s the Liverpool envy fizzed right down the M62. Those United v Liverpool fixtures became poisonous, but Liverpool got on fine with Manchester City and Leeds United fans. Why? They all found reason to despise United.

SRC: Look at the derby arm work I found in Sheffield. I just hope this fan's sleeve doesn't ride all the way up if he ever shakes hands with his rival.

The idea that you might you hate your local rival so much that you would even have their name tattooed right the way up your arm, smacks more of love and respect to me. After all, you end up going to bed every night sleeping with the name of your bitterest enemy inscribed on your body – and it's forever.

In at Number One (but without a bullet) in my chart of best derbies, is one most people have never heard of: Auchinleck Talbot v Cumnock Juniors in the West of Scotland, near where Bill Shankly was born. Okay, it's well below the radar of most people, teleprinters even, but years ago, at a meeting of the Football Trust, big Tom Wharton the giant of Scottish international refereeing, heard I was off to photograph at Auchinleck. He grimaced and told me: 'You'd better take your steel umbrella, laddie, hatred shall rain down upon thee.' Biblical Big Tom knew what he was talking about because he had refereed plenty of spicy Celtic-Rangers Old Firm games in his time. And he was indeed right. Before 90 minutes were up, there were rocks scattered all over the pitch from the humiliated Juniors' fans who were leaving the ground early, via the back alley.

JW: Football derbies can be a powerful stage for dramatizing political, ethnic or faith differences, but its strongest rivalries are often simply about geography

'A Loving Arm' - **Sheffield United at Sheffield Wednesday, 2012**
(SRC)

and localism. Burnley v Blackburn Rovers, for example, is a pretty intense local derby. All kinds of special arrangements are made to keep the peace. That pent-up East Lancashire macho pride has been nicely brewing and expressed around football for over 130 years. Some of these rival supporters can barely look at each other unsupervised.

SRC: Burnley actually advertises this fixture at Turf Moor as 'Burnley Vs -------' always leaving blank the opposition space because they know that the Claret fans would just tear down any mention of Rovers.

There are also derby rivalries which bring together very different types of town. In Lincolnshire where I live now – a bit of a Bermuda triangle for football success – we've got Scunthorpe (United) known for its iron and steel, Grimsby (Town) for its fishing industry, and Lincoln (City), which lays claim to an airborne heritage – that lofty cathedral – but also via its surrounding RAF airfields. Memories of Lancaster Bombers and Spitfires. At home matches at Lincoln's Sincil Bank today the old air raid siren is still wound up and the crowd loves it. We know already about the 'football fishing fleet' from Grimsby, with boats named after football clubs of the day including, incidentally, Real Madrid. This gave local men a sense of pride in their vessel and a competitive edge to try to out-catch, say, a GY702 Huddersfield Town trawler.

JW: Let's get back to dry land – indeed to landlocked land. Sadly, British football also has its many unrequited

'Liverpool Fans Cruelly Expose Manchester United' - at Aston Villa, 1990

(SRC)

derbies; those complicated local rivalries which can play out like the messiest of *ménage a trois*. In the East Midlands, for example, Leicester City fans like to eye up Nottingham Forest, European Cups and all. But Forest fans try to ignore Leicester – *their* derby is against Derby County, where they can argue the toss about who really owns the memory of Brian Clough. Westwards, just over the county line, Coventry City look on enviously. Can someone come and play with us? They dream of being Aston Villa's derby rivals, but the Holte End couldn't care less: they have the Blues in their own backyard to worry about. So each local meeting has its own juicy little sub plot. Why can't you loathe us as much as we loathe you?

SRC: Success also has a big part to play in the derby

dynamic. On my old patch, Carlisle United v Preston North End became a bit of an important derby for a while, as both clubs looked destined to push each other along, up the divisions. It could even become a happening event once more.

Just outside the Football League, FC United and Salford City are already trading some metaphorical blows – but landing more on other clubs as they both rip up the football pyramid. These are friendly clubs, I hasten to say. But others may envy their success – and come to dislike or hate them before any unhealthy admiration can set in. In football, the message seems to be that we all need someone to denigrate, to revile, if only to remind us who we are not.

CHAPTER 8

Obeying The Laws

'Border Incident' - **Burnley at Carlisle United, 1992**
(SRC)

'Stumbled Upon The Pitch' - **Carlisle United, 1992**
(SRC)

SRC: An amazing thing about British football is that you are just a few feet from multi-million pound players and multi-billion pound match-events and there is almost nothing to stop you striking out at a player, or running on the pitch and halting the game. But very few people do. In other countries they may need fences, moats, armed guards and snarling dogs to keep the fans at bay. We want none of that now. Believe it or not, I think we have become quite trusting of each other at British football.

JW: There are the laws of the game, and there are the laws beyond it, which smack of social lore. Some instructions have become real laws, like not invading the pitch (1991 onwards), but most things governing fan behaviour are unwritten laws – codes of conduct, really. Racist behaviour and racist chanting was made an offence by law, again in 1991, after the Taylor report. But to this day it's not wholly enforceable. Rather, it is down to the

people – the fans – not to be racist or homophobic and not to entertain hearing it from anyone else. It is hard to stop people having racist attitudes or to deal with individual instances of racism or homophobia inside the ground. But the anti-racist campaigns here in Britain have been pretty successful. Problems seem much worse abroad. I think the way the game has globalised here has also had a positive impact on fans in Britain. It's not easy shouting racist abuse when half the team you're supporting is recruited from around the world.

SRC: In Britain it's about trust, which goes hand in hand with freedom of speech. The police allow rival fans to be within shaking hands distance because most people respect the need to keep the atmosphere going in a genuine way. Authentic is what we do well.

JW: But that trust does break down occasionally, usually

'Shepherds Bush Telegram' - Queens Park Rangers at Cardiff, 2003
(SRC)

because fans get angry and frustrated at owners or officials. But Hillsborough did teach us about the dangers of policing and stewarding and the fatal risks of fencing – a very expensive lesson. Problems among some fans abroad seem to be growing, with re-emerging forms of extreme nationalism and intolerance often expressed at football. We can't discount it returning to the UK.

SRC: These changes have attracted more black British fans, so our football grounds are beginning to feel much more like who we really are today. Do you remember there used to be all those signs – quite comical actually

– outside grounds, which gave a list of the things you weren't allowed to take in? Smoke cannisters; guns; livestock, etc. But they didn't ever cover racist attitudes. Nor did they provide a picture prohibiting someone from violent swearing, like the signs you sometimes get in old public swimming pools.

JW: What about when players interact with fans? Not in an Eric Cantona way, but when players throw themselves into the crowd in celebration. Surely, we want a bit more of that in our game: moments full of cathartic love between players and supporters. At times like these, when you get

Liverpool v Everton at Anfield, September 1967
(Mirrorpix)

that mass celebratory hug on the touchline, it can seem as if the boundaries between players and fans really do dissolve a little. You can almost believe at such moments that footballers might even love the club as much as you do. At least, that is, until the next transfer window.

SRC: Referees often book players for this sort of ecstatic abandon: *dangerous and against the laws of the game*. But it might be more against the spirit of football to be quite so harsh. Perhaps we should book or send off any referee who is so boring as to just go by the letter of the law and stop the fun.

JW: These incidents are different from the determined pitch invaders, the guys who are uncontrollably angry, perhaps at the board, the referee, or poor Arsene Wenger. You can see why players and officials might be fearful about this kind of intrusion. Is he aimed at attacking me? Is he armed? Police or stewards chasing supporters onto the sacred turf can be a welcome and humorous distraction for fans. Will they catch him, or her? How many items of clothing can a fan successfully leave behind in the flailing hands of his pursuers? Will the invader get back into the crowd? Should we boo or cheer them?

SRC: For a while it became almost a requirement in this country that you had a sporting streaker: at football, rugby, and even at cricket. Are these 'soft' intruders treated differently from someone who invades the pitch with a bit more malice? I wouldn't be surprised if they eventually get let back into the ground, maybe wearing the groundsman's spare overcoat. It's: *Carry On Up The Football!*

There can also be a serious 'political' breaking of rules at football, a bit like the mass trespass on Kinder Scout in 1932 in the Peak District to protest at walkers being denied access to areas of open country. Sometimes, there may be no other way to put across a point than to demonstrate on, and off, the pitch. Coventry City pitch invaders at the Ricoh in 2016 were aiming to get their hopeless hedge fund owners SISU out and even the local police seemed to be supporting them. Other Sky Blues fans had earlier refused even to go into the ground. The club chairman responded by saying that organised pickets like there was a case of *lions being led by donkeys*. Naturally, the fans then dressed up as both. When Coventry City were sent down the M1 in the 2013/14 season to play 'home' games at Northampton Town, some City fans followed in their animal heads and gathered on a hill outside the stadium.

JW: Fancy dress at the season's end has become a new invented tradition at British football grounds. Supporters find it a bit more difficult to lose their heads if they are dressed up. But the FA, FIFA and UEFA don't like protests – breaking the rules – but protesting at football has definitely become more inventive, a lot more theatrical. And much more necessary.

SRC: Those protesting Coventry City supporters at Northampton look positively Shakespearean. But players and coaches can also be pulled up for supporting 'political' causes at matches. A forward can drag up his shirt to reveal a message that says he 'Loves Jesus', but not one that says the same about striking workers. Pep Guardiola's Catalonian yellow ribbon has also upset the FA recently.

JW: In the good old days, of course, local football protesters might have got their home-made placards out, At ground level today, a fan might not just get chucked out (but readmitted next match), but rather face a long term ban for a stunt like the one in the Everton handbag

'Donkeys And Lions Together In Protest'
Coventry City at Northampton Town, 2014
(SRC)

picture. Subtly, or not, supporters invariably drape stuff over the perimeter hoarding, including themselves. Which cheeses off the club's commercial director, sponsors and club partners. Today's supporters are more likely, instead, to club together and hire a small plane to deliver their complaint or 'joke'.

Meanwhile, owners and managers have become much more thin-skinned, more vulnerable in the media spotlight.

SRC: And to ram this home, there's Twitter: 'Sell our club Mr Ashley to someone who wants to be here before it's too late again' writes Alan Shearer on the social media platform where everyone, not just superstars, can have a pop at anyone they like, or dislike. Owners and managers wait for the next fan performance or intrusion, but rather than worry about this happening on or near the pitch, they are probably more worried about social media; they can never quite be sure if the law protecting freedom of speech is about to deliver an uncomfortable rude-awakening 280 character address to them. Even if they choose to ignore such *advice*, many, many others will see it.

JW: Who would be in charge of a football club in the internet age?

In 2019 there is a lengthy list of valued and historic English clubs – Port Vale, Coventry City, Bolton Wanderers and Blackpool among them – whose very future is very far from secure. Some owners seem so incompetent – or worse.

CHAPTER 9

A Game Of Modest Invention

SRC: The game is often said in casual conversation to have 'changed beyond all recognition'. But I don't think it has – not on the pitch at least. Its simplicity is still its charm. Instinctively, I think we know that the game is pretty much how we want it to be. If there are any changes to be made, they are usually made grudgingly, gradually, increment by increment.

1959 Advert for the oldest sports brand in the world, relaunched as Mitre
(Mirrorpix)

JW: I would say that football adapted quickly right at the start. Initially, players could catch the ball – but not run with it – and the early game under FA laws still had scrimmages, mass pile-ups to try to force the ball forward. As the use of the hands for outfield players disappeared and football became more competitive and more professional, we needed neutral referees to deal with fouls and contentious decisions. Ex-public-school players were unhappy. They argued that no true gentlemen could commit fouls, so they abhorred the awarding of penalty kicks as an attack on their character. Upper class footballers might miss spot

kicks on purpose, just to make a point.

We had the revised offside law in 1925, of course – which led to more goals and a new defensive position, the stopper centre-half. But I suppose the role of the goalkeeper has changed most over time. Keepers get a bit more protection now compared to the days when they got kicked around and barged into the net. Goalkeepers could handle the ball (but not run with it) anywhere in their own half until 1912. Leigh Roose, a Welsh goalkeeper, liked to bounce the ball (and his opponents) outside his area and when he retired the law change was made.

Bournemouth and Boscombe's Jack Bradford, 1930
(Mirrorpix)

SRC: It took another 80 years, though, for football's leaders to decide that it was a bad idea to let keepers handle back-passes from defenders in trouble.

JW: Goalkeepers are a little less detached from their

'The Inswinging Corner Kicker' - **Stockport County, 1990**
(SRC)

lace imprint. If heading does go from the game – it's already banned for kids in the USA – say goodbye, too, to the British corner and long throw specialists. No more jumping around at the ball (and opponents) in the penalty box, so much a part of the British game.

SRC: When you think about it, the throw-in has always been a bit of an anomaly in football. You have this fantastic, high skill game all about keeping the ball moving by preventing the use of the hands – sheer genius. But when the ball goes out of play on the sidelines you allow it to be picked up and *thrown* back in. Why? You take a corner *kick*, so why a throw? Nevertheless, these restarts do require specialist skills. The shape players have to get into to take long throw-ins and deliver swinging corners, their balance and flexibility, is incredible.

team-mates these days and the notion that if you couldn't play you got stuck in goal has long disappeared. Today's keepers need to be as smart with their feet as they are with their hands and Pep's way at Manchester City is a new version of 'total football' where even the man between the sticks is super slick at passing the ball outside his own area.

SRC: And what about heading? I think it's almost over for 'heading a ball'. Alan Shearer has spent a year, now that his footballing career is over, looking into this, fearing what may lay ahead for him and the current crop of players. There are so many cases of ex-players having dementia. Balls of almost any fabric, except beach balls, when at speed are much like missiles to the head.

Incidentally, I myself often get hit on the back of the head when busy photographing the crowd with my back to the pitch. Paul Gascoigne (Gazza) warming up for Spurs at Millwall, knocked me clean out from 30 yards away. His goalie, Erik Thorstvedt, genuinely concerned, picked me up and looked me in the eyes; over his shoulder, in the distance, I could just about see Gazza grinning from ear to ear. The Millwall crowd loved it. Footballer 1 Photographer/Paparazzo 0.

JW: You do know that wingers were supposedly rated by old-school centre-forwards by how well they could present a sodden leather football so that it could be headed cleanly, away from the ball's laces? Otherwise, it was a Saturday night out for the No.9 with an ugly facial

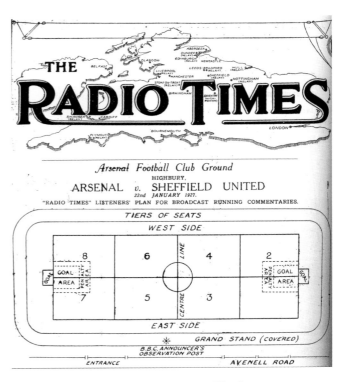

BBC Radio Times coverage to help listeners follow the game, 1927
(Mirrorpix)

JW: The throw-in probably came from the sport in the public schools when handling and kicking were both still allowed. Taking a threatening corner kick today is not an easy skill. Coaches demand much more. Look at the number of corners that are floated in, over-hit or don't

*Gravesend and Northfleet training session in the snow, ahead of their
FA Cup fourth round replay match at Sunderland 1963*
(Mirrorpix)

even get past the first defender. At night, under lights, a corner can sometimes seem like a lonely delivery into the unknown. Where are your targets, your team- mates? Is anybody out there?

SRC: Fans abroad are always intrigued by the British response to being awarded a corner. We get really excited, our centre-backs piling in with the forwards and then the usual argy-bargy starts in the box. Pure theatre. But in the continent, getting a corner is not quite such a big deal, just another means of restarting play. At Barcelona, they like taking corners short, as if it is rather vulgar to try to score by simply pumping the ball into the area. According to Opta, only 4% of Premier League corners result directly in goals. So why get so excited? We do, anyway.

JW: One major change in our thinking about football came when broadcasting came along. We did then have to 're-invent' the game for people who were not in the stadium (we just might be doing the same in 2018 with VAR). So, when the BBC started broadcasting matches live on the radio in 1927, the broadcasters tried to make the game more meaningful for people at home by providing, in the *Radio Times*, a helpful grid guide to the pitch.

SRC: So, this was another modest adjustment, one helping to communicate the game to a wider public.

Listeners checked out the grid whilst listening to the commentator. In the background, an assistant was navigating you around the field by shouting out square numbers.

JW: It sounds crazy, I know, but it's actually quite a clever idea, much ridiculed since. When you listen to football on the radio now, can you ever really work out what's going on, or exactly where the play is? I doubt it. The saying, 'Back to square one' might have come from these first radio football commentaries. Sounds plausible to me. Listening to football on the radio allows for your imagination to do most of the work – and you can also feed the cat or wash the car at the same time.

If the game hasn't changed all that much on the pitch itself, then what about preparations off it? Just as television has begun to master broadcast coverage – 24 camera angles in the Sky Sports revolution – so the players and coaches and legions of analysts started to make a beeline to monitors and graphics to review their own performance and the form of the opposition. A step up from Don Revie's old dossiers and bingo cards in the 1960s.

*Bill Shankly and his young Huddersfield Town players,
training on rough ground, 1st May 1959*
(Mirrorpix)

Historically, preparing players was rarely very sophisticated in British football. We saw it as a straightforward game, combining perspiration with natural talent. Training to play meant being shouted at by ex-military men, rather like those infantrymen bounding

West Ham goalkeeper Standen dives at the feet of Bobby Charlton to prevent a goalscoring opportunity. Manchester United 0 v West Ham United 1, October 1963
(Mirrorpix)

out of the trenches. No need for complex coaching or tactical schooling.

SRC: The Gravesend players featured here, pictured training in the snow and hamming it up for the FA Cup cameras in the 1960s, probably had nowhere else to practice their moves and certainly not a gym or a leisure complex to work in. Today, Brighton & Hove Albion and several other clubs stay overnight at St. Georges Park, the new home of Team England, on the way to various away games. There they can use every piece of technology and fitness equipment known to sport.

JW: The British game is chock-full of stories of tanner ball players with God-given talent and old-style club trainers who told their less gifted men: 'No need for work with the ball this week. You can get hungry for that at the weekend.' British football has always been seen as a bit

of a battle, more brawn than brains, more desire than tactics. Even the visionary Bill Shankly had Denis Law and his Huddersfield Town team-mates training on a car park when times were hard. When he moved to Liverpool, Shanks had his young players playing training matches against local bin men.

SRC: Around the same time that Shankly was playing games in car parks there was a great leap forward in the use of photographs to help tell the story of the match.

There is an action shot at Old Trafford in the early 1960s which feels to me like a very traditional English football scene on a typical winter's day in industrial Manchester. The floodlight pylon echoes the factory chimney, so the industrial roots of the game seem especially clear in this picture. It also shows the intensity and physicality that's still so important to the British – this goalkeeper is about to risk real injury here, possibly a boot in the face. We can also see in the foreground another photographer to the one taking the picture, doing his job, included as part of the event. This is quite an arty composition.

Today at matches photographers are usually given bibs with numbers on them and I am always mindful about the number on my back. I see myself as a player of sorts: a DH Lawrence-style 'go-between', someone who links the match on the pitch with the crowd and their experience off it. Do I want to be a number nine, or a number seven, or even a number one? At World Cups, such is the scope of the event and the international media demand that my number has sometimes run into the hundreds.

Sports photographers around the time of the *Bobby Charlton-about-to-boot-the-ball-and-goalie-into-the-net* real action shot, started using telephoto lenses, which meant that they could appear to get closer to the action, whilst not actually being quite so close. You could now photograph goalmouth action from up the other end of the pitch – the goalie lying injured after a clash with Charlton, or an incident involving a skinhead in the crowd. Photographers could now do all of this from far away, from a safe distance. And, of course, without having the faintest idea what was truly going on.

'The Singing Stand' - West Bromwich Albion, 1994
(SRC)

certainly at the highest level. 'Text me' says someone who may be stood only a few feet away. And yet social media can give the impression of a new kind of direct connection to the stars.

Twitter can offer an idea of what goes on behind the scenes, but it is a very managed picture. How can we get a look behind the curtain? In Manchester City's exclusive new Tunnel Club, corporate fans can now watch that sacred moment before the game when players are twitching and eyeing up the opposition in the players' tunnel.

SRC: For photographers, once colour arrived in the 1960s the use of black and white film lent the subject a certain kind of artistic depth. One of reserve, of distance – of another time. Colour is the stuff of cheap polaroids and family albums, something you owned yourself rather than something the photographer showed you. Newspapers typically told the story in black-and-white, shades which were beyond most people's emotions and experience.

JW: I guess you could say that in the last 30 years or so in England we have seen an increasing 'colouring-in' of the game and a softening of its outline. Some might even say we've been 'feminising' English football culture, making the sport progressively more accessible to others.

As top clubs have monetised the brand, that process has created a commercial energy but also a warmth inside stadiums, rather than chasing the more authentic, but sometimes hostile, conditions of the past. We are in that

Elton John superstar leading Watford FC
out for training at Vicarage Road, April 1974
(Mirrorpix)

JW: Over time, fans' relationships with photographers and the media has changed in complex ways, whilst links between fans and players have become ever more distant. That intimacy of meeting for a beer after a game with a top player in the local pub has pretty much gone,

Sunderland framework all ready for the new stand being erected at the Fulwell end of Roker Park, July 1964
(Mirrorpix)

second generation of the 'family atmosphere' and greater inclusivity inside English grounds – which is, itself, an invention.

SRC: I would say some of that began much earlier at my own club, Watford, with Graham Taylor back in the late 70s. Vicarage Road went from being a few blokes dotted about on crumbling terraces (I remember a guy in a string vest we called 'The Man with The Bag' pacing about yelling, and always threatening to leave) to becoming a club and a ground which was much more welcoming. It was a place that came with a certain Elton John attached. The chairman's aura – even when he was not physically there – somehow filled a void. He seemed to colour the place gold and black, thus lifting drab, little Watford. Football stands began to be named after sponsors but also after people who had made clubs into what they were. People like Graham Taylor. For good or ill, labels such as East, West, South, North, Kop and Enclosure would largely be confined to history as grounds were rebuilt.

JW: Your memories about Watford FC are a very useful reminder to me that if you look back through the 1960s and 1970s with too much nostalgia you realise that lots of stands at football grounds were at best functional and at worst pretty shabbily constructed. For every classic Archibald Leitch design from the past or careful later additions to his themes, there were football grounds which had some individuality but were also architecturally pretty uninspiring.

SRC: In the post-Hillsborough redevelopment phase for British football stadia, we now had a new colour palette and computer technology was widely available to us. I would say that we did have some examples which reconnected good design with the necessary art of putting a roof over fans' heads.

An obvious example was the new stadium for Huddersfield Town. I was able to photograph throughout the building process, which saw Town's historic Leeds Road ground (where the club won its league titles back in the 1930s) make way in 1994 for a revolutionary new, banana-roofed structure. Fans could watch it grow. I remember the local excitement when this amazing stadium started to sprout up – and in what most people had dismissed as just a humble northern town that had seen better days.

Even when it was only half-completed, it was voted RIBA's 1995 best new building of the year. Not just the best new *sports* building, but the best new *building* of any kind. What a feather in the cap for the club and the game. When it opened, you had a real sense of being part of something truly inspirational for the north.

'East Corner Fortune' - Rangers, 1992
(SRC)

JW: The 1990s were important because, although I think we built too many 'identikit' stadia, new grounds with far too little imagination, style or identity of their own, the period also demonstrated that designing a new football ground could be prestigious and a source of civic pride once more. Herbert Chapman, himself, probably stirred

'New Home On The Horizon' - Huddersfield Town, 1994
(SRC)

when In 2018 that Huddersfield stadium was at last where it could best be admired – in the Premier League.

SRC: Which brings us, finally, on to the biggest recent 'invention' for the elite English game, the mega-money satellite TV deals which brought 'live' Premier League football to millions in the UK and hundreds of millions more worldwide. Satellite TV's dynamic would challenge the power of the turnstiles and gate receipts as the main wealth-supplier for top clubs. Television had to get people to see the game its way – to crack the long-standing ritual of 3pm Saturday kick-offs, for example – in favour of

broadcast football every night of the week.

JW: Who would ever have imagined that on a Monday night, at a time when most fans would be reflecting on what their team had done at the weekend, we would all be directed to watch yet *another* live game at home or in the pub? On one recent weekend in February 2018 the sports TV stations offered fans in Britain a reported 23 live matches from all over Europe. Will we keep on wanting to go to stadiums in the future as live football spreads on TV? I wonder.

CHAPTER 10

Final Score (Well Almost)

'Holding Back Time' - **Clydebank, 1995**
(SRC)

broadcasters, an opportunity to dissect the match so far – and cram in the requisite adverts. One way the game has certainly changed at the top level is the computer-aided half-time expert analysis, but also the messing about with kick-off times. It was so much simpler when everyone kicked off at the same time, on the same day. In the days when all matches kicked off at 3pm on Saturdays and finished around ten-to-five, sports newspaper men lived on their nerves. Most football grounds didn't even have a clock back then, so it was almost complete guesswork for fans (and editors) when games would end.

'Scoreboard's Winter Cheer' - **Shrewsbury Town, 1991**
(SRC)

JW: We are over half-way through our conversations. It feels right that we have a chapter at this point, about the ritual of time itself, and its interruption. Times have changed, we say, as if we are heading towards something else. Something better? Something later? After half-time? A reckoning time?

SRC: What is it about half-time at a football match? The commentators often say about managers that they can 'hardly wait' to get their players in the dressing-room, as if something magical can happen there. More importantly, it's as if half-time can actually stop time in its tracks. A chance to reset the clock, put things right.

JW: For the players and coaches it is a chance to recalibrate. Where is it going wrong? What do we need to do to hold on? Managers can later use the half-time message to keep their own mystique alive. For fans, it's time for a leg-stretch and maybe a pee and a pie. For

SRC: At Clydebank there was something really novel: a guy whose role was no less than to 'hold back time' with a big stick until the referee started the game. Earlier, the same guy had been organizing the car park, directing traffic, a jack of all trades. Holding back time was just one of his many matchday jobs.

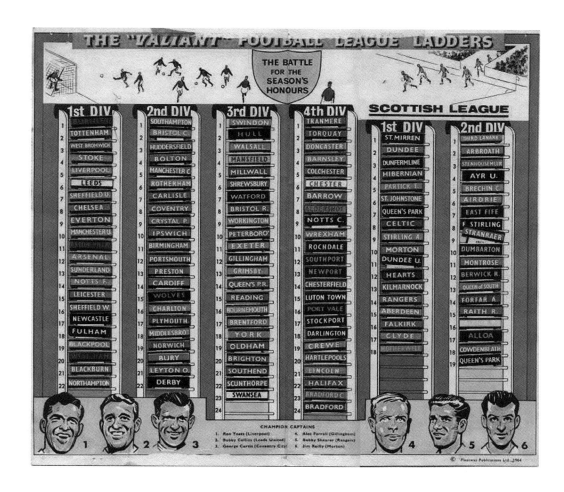

The Valiant Football League Ladders, 1965-66

JW: That is quite a talent. At half-time, before mobile phones intervened and when every match kicked off at three o'clock, there would also be round-ups of all the scores around the grounds. The men inside their strange old ABCDEF huts had one eye on the pitch and their ear to BBC radio. How quickly can we get the half-times out? Or else you watched stewards walk slowly around the pitch carrying the score numbers to pin next to the half-time letters listed only in the match programme. 'Is he carrying a five? Who can be five down at half-time?' 'Which match is D?' You could hear the crowd gasp as an outlier score went up: 'Shrewsbury beating Watford 4-1! At half-time!' The buzz would go around all the grounds.

SRC: Scoreboards really only grabbed you for a few minutes around half time. Once you got tuned into the important national developments the scoreboard attendants could get back to watching their own match, and with a grandstand view. I think this connecting up of all these local skirmishes to the national football battle was part of the enjoyment of everyone playing at the same time. Afterwards, the *Evening Pink* or *Football Green* newspapers were printed all around the country with match reports, results on the front page and late scores in the Stop Press. All this within 30 minutes of matches ending. How did they do it?

JW: My dad used to send me out to get the pink *Football Echo* on Saturday evenings in Liverpool. Queues of working men outside local newsagents and sweet shops. If Everton had been at home they would get the front-page story, Liverpool the back. Blazing headlines were routinely in play: *'Reds/Blues see off Gunners/Hammers.'* Our smaller regional neighbours, Tranmere Rovers, Southport, Wrexham and Chester would all have their own short match reports. A bit of rugby league - Liverpool City, St. Helens and Wigan - was on the back page. You could tell what had happened in the big local games because there was always a little drawing of a Kopite (Liverpool) and a Toffee Lady (Everton) at the top of the front page. They would dance wildly if their team had won, be downcast in defeat, or hold a point on a flat hand for a draw. A little bit of cartoon magic for the kids.

'Reporters On Laptops And Urn Of Tea' - **Sunderland, 1991**
(SRC)

SRC: For those supporters not walking to the game, but who instead had legged it back to the car to tune into the radio, another matchday tradition awaited. Bang on 5pm on Saturday - and it's still happening now, complete with same piece of music that has accompanied it for generations - is the reading on the BBC of the Classified Football Results. (There was something very definitive about that word 'classified'). For 40 years, the results were read by James Alexander Gordon, with his lovely Scottish brogue. Now, (revolution is here) a woman, Charlotte Green is in charge on BBC radio, who has an equally soothing, but authoritative, voice. Voice pitch *up* for a winning score, down for a defeat. Level it out for the spoils shared. Charlotte's nailed it. Despite the Sky and BT alternatives, this ritual still tells us about places in Britain that we have never visited or ever imagined.

How could we know anything about them if it wasn't

for the national football scores, read out every Saturday at 5pm? Every senior club's name is still in there, fed into and spewed out by the BBC teleprinter using what seemed at the time like amazing and puzzling technology.

Recently, just when you think the scores have finally ended at some exotic and mysterious location in Scotland, a Stenhousemuir or a Stranraer, the Welsh Premier League scores pop up. Devolution times. There is that feeling, especially in winter, that the whole nation was wrapped up in the same itchy, but warming, woolly blanket - of football.

JW: Look, things have moved on and complainers about change usually also love all the additional live football on TV today. So, let's try to rein in some of this nostalgia, because that's what it is. But you definitely did feel part of something which was widely shared back then - a nation's Saturday heartbeat - something that was being replicated, in real time, all over the country. As kids, we messed about with those 'high tech' card football table ladders, which were given away free in comics. I dare say all this is done much better online now. And people also knew, back then, that you had your weekends clearly laid out. Saturdays for football; Sundays free for family time: walk the car, wash the dog, sell the kids. No internet or mobiles meant that match reporters were vital for most people's basic football information - yet they worked to punitive deadlines and in pretty primitive conditions.

SRC: The photograph of these press men at Sunderland was taken in the early 90s, when we were on the very cusp of major change. They have early laptops, but not the internet. It was still called 'the wire' back then, a form of telegram service. It's a homely image - check the carpet - even though the match was in fact a big one, Sunderland v Arsenal. The photograph from the press box at Kilmarnock I especially like because this reporter looks like a spy phoning in his latest findings.

Today, of course, everyone is a reporter, fans tweeting out comments as the game goes on, later ringing in the phone-in shows, usually enraged. You can see every goal online and some supporters even run their own little TV stations. But before the 2000s we all hung on the written words of that gallant small gang of football press journalists. They probably spoke their account of games down a telephone line to a secretary, who didn't necessarily dig football, but typed it all up anyway. Today, the press pack is able to send their pictures and words

'Filing The Match Report' - **Kilmarnock, 1996**
(SRC)

from a ground in a flash. We can also hear their views in seconds (if we really want to). And, whisper it, there are now even some *female* reporters.

JW: Spending time in the Premier League is what dictates exactly who wants to receive your message these days. How large is your prospective fan base today, how many supporters do you need to try to get your stories to? Information is money. And to some extent the clubs boss it: the British newspaper is no longer number one for club news. The clubs call the tune despite the fact that hundreds of thousands of people also want to (and do) weigh into the conversation. Some fan bloggers can have audiences reaching hundreds of thousands, and what the

TV pundits do or say is immediately part of the football story today, especially if they mess up somehow.

Top clubs churn out millions of PR stories and they and their sponsors try to control much more of what their players say. Journalists have to pick at what scraps of 'original' material they can get hold of. Everyone else has an opinion these days – and, apparently, we all have to listen to them. 'Experts' no longer hold sway and nobody tells us what has *really* happened on the field, not even VAR! We are all expected to make our own judgements – the game is 'all about opinions' as some idiotic pundits insist. It could be seen as a form of democratization, but I'm not sure we wouldn't be better back with those ABC half-time scoreboards.

Football's Timeline

OVER 200 MOMENTOUS YEARS IN BRITISH HISTORY

WITH mitre

1817 Benjamin Crook opens his tannery in Huddersfield, so the oldest sports brand in the world is founded - which later becomes MITRE

1845 The first written 'football' rules are produced by three pupils at Rugby School

1848 The Cambridge rules follow, with goal kicks, throw-ins and forward passes

1857 Sheffield FC is formed, with claims to be the world's first football club

1862 Notts County FC is founded in the George Hotel in Nottingham, and are thus the oldest surviving professional football club in the world

1863 In London, meetings between ex-public-school men results in the world's first Football Association ('The FA') and some national laws for football

1866 Forward passing is accepted in the national laws.

1871 A split in the FA ranks produces the Rugby Football Union for a game mainly played using the hands

1872 Wanderers FC beat Royal Engineers in the first FA Cup final, at the Kennington Oval. Scotland play England in a 0-0 draw in the world's first international fixture

1875 The introduction of a crossbar to replace tape between two poles is approved

1876 25th March: Wales plays its first international match, a 4-0 loss against Scotland in Partick

1878 Newton Heath Lancashire & Yorkshire Railway FC is established, later to become Manchester United. Everton FC are also formed and move to play at Anfield in 1884. A dispute among the club's directors in 1892 will lead to the formation of Liverpool FC - and the departure of Everton to nearby Goodison Park

1881 The Scot Andrew Watson becomes the world's first black football international

1882 The four Home associations meet in Manchester in December to try to agree an early uniform set of rules/laws for playing football across national borders

1883 31st March: Blackburn Olympic become the first northern working-class club to win the FA Cup. No ex-public school club will triumph again

1884 The first FA Amateur Cup final is staged in response to the increasing domination of the sport by professional clubs. Old Carthusians beat Casuals 2-1 at the Athletic Ground

1885 The FA is forced to legalise professionalism after complaints from southern clubs about northern professionals in the FA Cup

1886 The International Football Association Board (IFAB) is established and it now guards the new international laws of the game

1887 The IFAB approves two major law changes. The duration of the match shall be 90 minutes and games should be played by 11 players on each side

1888 William McGregor, an Aston Villa director, leads on the formation of the 12-club Football League

1889 Preston North End, becomes the first club to win the Football League/FA Cup double

1890 Stoke become the first Football League club to fail to get re-elected, joining the Football Alliance, which they won and thus were re-elected to the Football League

1891 The goal net, referees and penalty kicks (the 'kick of death') are all introduced into the game

1894 Nettie Honeyball persuades 30 young women to join the first British Ladies Football Club

1895 23rd March: The first officially recorded women's match takes place, at Crouch End, London

1898 Automatic promotion and relegation for two clubs is introduced into the two division Football League

1899 Darwen FC establish the league record for the most consecutive losses in a single season, 18

1900 Bury FC beat Southampton 4-0 in the FA Cup final at Crystal Palace. The club's directors promised players a £10 bonus for a win. Three years later Bury were back to defeat Derby County by a record 6-0 score. Two finals, two wins and a remarkable 10-0 aggregate score-line

1901 Under FA strictures, the Football League introduces a maximum wage for players of £4 per week into its regulations. Tottenham Hotspur become the first and only non-league club to win the FA Cup after the formation of the Football League

1902 5th April: The first major stadium disaster in British football, at Ibrox Park, Glasgow, kills 25 spectators

1904 The Fédération Internationale de Football Association (FIFA) is founded in Paris

1907 The PFA is convened in Manchester originally as the Association of Football Players' & Trainers' Union

1908 6th June: England's first international match against foreign opposition, a 6-1 victory in Austria

1909 Goalkeepers must now wear a shirt (a jersey) that is distinguishable from all the other players and the match officials

1911 Founded only in 1903 and immediately elected into the Football League Second Division, Bradford City win the FA Cup, still the club's only major honour

1912 The laws prohibit goalkeepers from handling the ball outside the penalty area; previously, they could handle the ball anywhere in their own half

1914 The King attends the FA Cup final for the first time. As war breaks out in August, the Football League decides to play on, to official consternation

1915 1st January 1915: A letter written by a doctor attached to the Rifle Brigade, is published in The Times, reporting on a football match played by British and German troops between the trenches in France. 2nd April: A Football League match between Liverpool and Manchester United is fixed by players on both sides

1917 The Dick Kerr's Ladies club is formed in Preston, the most important of the early women's clubs

1919 As football reboots, the First Division is expanded from 20 to 22 clubs. Mysteriously Tottenham Hotspur, 20th in 1915, are not re-elected. Instead, rivals Arsenal, 5th in the Second Division, are promoted, some sources allege via bribes

1920 Leading clubs from the Southern League join the Football League to form a new Third Division

1921 The wartime popularity of women's football leads The FA to ban women's clubs at its members' grounds

1922 From the 1922/23 league season, re-election is required of the bottom two clubs of both the Third Division North and Third Division South

1923 28th April: The first Wembley FA Cup final sees chaotic scenes as the pitch is overrun by fans

1924 Herbert Chapman wins the First Division title for the first time, as manager of Huddersfield Town. The Town would go on to win three titles in a row, the first club to do so

1925 The offside law is changed from three to two players, thus producing more goals

1927 23rd April: Cardiff City are the first and only non-English club to win the FA Cup, beating Arsenal 1-0. Another Welsh outfit, Aberdare Athletic, fail to get re-elected into the Football League, being replaced by Torquay United

1928 Everton's Dixie Dean becomes the first player to score 60 top flight league goals in one season. No one since has matched the feat

1930 21st April: Leicester City and Arsenal draw 6-6, still the highest scoring draw at the top level in England

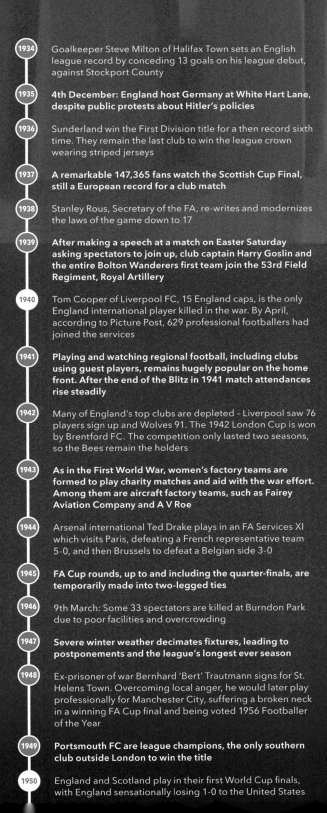

1934 Goalkeeper Steve Milton of Halifax Town sets an English league record by conceding 13 goals on his league debut, against Stockport County

1935 4th December: England host Germany at White Hart Lane, despite public protests about Hitler's policies

1936 Sunderland win the First Division title for a then record sixth time. They remain the last club to win the league crown wearing striped jerseys

1937 A remarkable 147,365 fans watch the Scottish Cup Final, still a European record for a club match

1938 Stanley Rous, Secretary of the FA, re-writes and modernizes the laws of the game down to 17

1939 After making a speech at a match on Easter Saturday asking spectators to join up, club captain Harry Goslin and the entire Bolton Wanderers first team join the 53rd Field Regiment, Royal Artillery

1940 Tom Cooper of Liverpool FC, 15 England caps, is the only England international player killed in the war. By April, according to Picture Post, 629 professional footballers had joined the services

1941 Playing and watching regional football, including clubs using guest players, remains hugely popular on the home front. After the end of the Blitz in 1941 match attendances rise steadily

1942 Many of England's top clubs are depleted - Liverpool saw 76 players sign up and Wolves 91. The 1942 London Cup is won by Brentford FC. The competition only lasted two seasons, so the Bees remain the holders

1943 As in the First World War, women's factory teams are formed to play charity matches and aid with the war effort. Among them are aircraft factory teams, such as Fairey Aviation Company and A V Roe

1944 Arsenal international Ted Drake plays in an FA Services XI which visits Paris, defeating a French representative team 5-0, and then Brussels to defeat a Belgian side 3-0

1945 FA Cup rounds, up to and including the quarter-finals, are temporarily made into two-legged ties

1946 9th March: Some 33 spectators are killed at Burndon Park due to poor facilities and overcrowding

1947 Severe winter weather decimates fixtures, leading to postponements and the league's longest ever season

1948 Ex-prisoner of war Bernhard 'Bert' Trautmann signs for St. Helens Town. Overcoming local anger, he would later play professionally for Manchester City, suffering a broken neck in a winning FA Cup final and being voted 1956 Footballer of the Year

1949 Portsmouth FC are league champions, the only southern club outside London to win the title

1950 England and Scotland play in their first World Cup finals, with England sensationally losing 1-0 to the United States

1952 After title disappointments in the previous five seasons, Manchester United finally end a 41-year wait for the First Division title, finishing four points ahead of rivals, Tottenham Hotspur and Arsenal

1953 25th November, in the 'Match of the Century', England loses its first fixture at Wembley, 6-3 to incomparable Hungary. Stanley Matthews finally wins an FA Cup winners medal, as Blackpool defeat Bolton Wanderers, 4-3

1954 23rd May: a confident England seek revenge in Budapest – and this time lose by a record 7-1 score

1955 Chelsea win the league title for the first time, but are refused permission by the Football League to compete in the new European Cup competition

1956 Manchester United, under Matt Busby, ignore the Football League and become the first British club to play in the European Cup

1957 Sunderland AFC are fined £5,000 by the FA for under the counter payments to players

1958 6th February: Manchester United's plane crashes at Munich airport, killing 23, including eight players

1959 Bill Shankly joins Liverpool FC, from Huddersfield Town, as manager: an epoch begins

1960 The new Football League Cup is launched: Aston Villa defeat Rotherham United 3-2 in a two-legged final

1961 The £20 maximum wage cap is lifted: Johnny Haynes becomes England's first £100 a week footballer

1962 26th December: Brian Clough retires through injury to become one of England's greatest ever club managers

1963 15th May Tottenham Hotspur win Britain's first European trophy, the European Cup Winners Cup, defeating Atletico Madrid 5-1 in Rotterdam

1964 The BBC TV football highlights show Match of the Day is launched. It continues to thrill and inform today. Three Sheffield Wednesday players are convicted of match fixing

1965 21st August: Keith Peacock of Charlton Athletic becomes the first substitute used in the Football League

1966 30th July: England win the World Cup at Wembley by defeating West Germany 4-2, after extra time

1967 25th May: Glasgow Celtic are the first British club to win the European Cup, defeating Inter Milan 2-1 in Lisbon. No other Scottish club would match this feat

1968 29th May: Manchester United win the European Cup, the first champions from England and just ten years after the tragedy of Munich

1969 The Women's Football Association (WFA) is formed and 44 clubs attend its inaugural meeting

1970 7th February: George Best scores a record six FA Cup goals

1971 2nd January: The Ibrox Stadium disaster – a horrific 66 fatalities, people crushed on a stairwell at a Rangers v Celtic match - completely overshadows Southampton winning the first Mitre Women's FA Cup

1972 18th November: The first official UK women's full international match sees Scotland 2, England 3, at Greenock

1973 17th October: For the first time, England fail to qualify for the World Cup finals, losing 1-0 to Poland

1974 Tottenham Hotspur receive a two-home game ban from UEFA after the club's fans riot in Holland

1975 The Anglo-Scottish Cup is launched to replace the unloved Texaco Cup

1976 Future England boss, the 32-year-old Graham Taylor, achieves the first success of his managerial career by winning the Fourth Division title with Lincoln City. He surprises all by taking over at Elton John's Watford, still in the Fourth Division – but they will soon be on the rise

1977 25th May: Liverpool win the European Cup in Rome, sparking a period of English successes in Europe

1978 Aberdeen FC boast Britain's first all-seated football stadium, at Pittodrie. 29th November 1978: Viv Anderson, the 22-year-old Nottingham Forest defender, becomes England's first black full international when he appears in the 1-0 friendly win over Czechoslovakia at Wembley

1979 30th May: Nottingham Forest's remarkable run under Brian Clough continues when they beat Malmö of Sweden 1-0 in the European Cup final, record signing Trevor Francis scoring the only goal

1980 1st March: Everton lose 2-1 at home to Liverpool in the Merseyside derby, and during the game legendary former striker Dixie Dean dies from a heart attack in the stands, aged 72

1981 Three points for a win is introduced, and QPR becomes the first club in Britain to install an artificial pitch

1982 Unbeaten England are still eliminated from the World Cup in Spain, as Northern Ireland beat the hosts

1983 Tottenham Hotspur form a holding company to evade FA restrictions on profits and directors' salaries

1984 Liverpool FC win a historic treble of trophies: the league title, the League Cup and the European Cup

1985 The Bradford fire and the Heysel Stadium disaster in Brussels signals British football's darkest year yet. League attendances the following season will slump to a post-war low of 16.5m

1986 Alex Ferguson joins Manchester United as manager: 38 trophies follow in 26 years at Old Trafford

1987 Burnley FC stave off a final day relegation from the Football League, thus extending their 99 years of membership, and promising a later return to the top flight

1988 Scunthorpe United build the first new purpose-built Football League stadium in England for 33 years

1989 15th April: The Hillsborough disaster means the deaths of 96 Liverpool fans at an FA Cup semi-final

1990 Liverpool's long domestic dominance is over, as heavy underdogs Crystal Palace defeat the Reds in a turbulent FA Cup semi-final at Villa Park

1991 The FA publishes its Blueprint for Football sanctioning, in 1992, a breakaway FA Premier League

1992 The FA Premier League is founded on the back of satellite TV money. The UEFA Champions League is also launched to replace the old knock out European Cup competition

1993 Manchester United become the first Premier League champions, while ending a 26-year title wait. Huddersfield Town move from run-down Leeds Road to the impressive new Alfred McAlpine Stadium at Kirklees, an early symbol of the regeneration of the English game

1994 Tottenham Hotspur are docked 5 points and found guilty of financial irregularities dating back to the 1980s. A proposed points deduction and FA Cup ban are eventually quashed on appeal

1995 The Bosman ruling allows players in the EU to move at the end of a contract without a transfer fee

1996 Arsene Wenger arrives at Arsenal, to manage 1,235 games over 22 years - and transform the English game. 22nd December: Peter Shilton, at Leyton Orient FC, becomes the first footballer to make 1,000 league appearances in English football

1997 A unique season for Middlesbrough FC. Runners-up in both domestic cup finals, they are relegated from the top level after player illness means they fail to fulfill a league fixture against Blackburn Rovers

1998 The Scottish Premier League is founded, breaking away from the Scottish Football League

1999 26th December: Chelsea FC fields the first starting XI in top level English football to contain no British players. 8th May: Carlisle United goalkeeper Jimmy Glass makes history by scoring the 95th minute goal that keeps his club in the Football League

2000 The FA Cup final will not involve the holders, Manchester United, who withdraw from the 1999–2000 competition to play in the FIFA Club World Championship in South America, thus becoming the first FA Cup winners not to defend their title

2001 Alex Ferguson, at Manchester United, becomes the first manager ever to win three successive English league titles

2002 The collapse of debt-ridden ITV Digital in May, plunges Football League clubs into crisis. Bradford City, Nottingham Forest, Watford, Barnsley, Lincoln City and Port Vale all file for administration, fearful that the drastic revenue loss might put them out of business

2003 Wimbledon FC relocates to Milton Keynes after controversially receiving permission to do so from the FA

2004 Arsenal are the first elite English club since 1889 to complete an entire league campaign unbeaten

2005 FC United of Manchester are formed by fans to protest the ownership of MUFC by the Glazer family from the USA. 25th May: Liverpool FC stage the most dramatic European final comeback in history to draw 3-3 with AC Milan in the Champions League, before winning the trophy on penalties

2006 Reading FC are promoted to the top flight for the first time in their history, after topping the Championship with a record 106 points

2007 More Americans, Tom Hicks and George Gillett, buy Liverpool FC, bringing debt and later fan protests before the courts finally remove the owners in 2010

2008 For the first time, two English clubs fight out the Champion's League final, as Manchester United beat Chelsea on penalties. Manchester City are taken over by the Abu Dhabi United Group, transforming them into one of the world's wealthiest football clubs

2009 28th March: Frank Lampard scores the 500th England goal at Wembley in a 4-0 win over Slovakia

2010 Portsmouth FC go into administration, the first Premier League club to do so, guaranteeing their relegation

2011 Sky Sports TV's flagship presenters, Richard Keys and Andy Gray, are sacked for making crude, sexist remarks, off air in the Sky studio

2012 13th May: Newly monied Manchester City score two stoppage time goals to snatch its first league title since 1968

2013 Football League 2 club Bradford City astonishes the professional game by reaching the League Cup final, the first fourth tier club to do so since Rochdale in 1962

2014 Fara Williams, once homeless, becomes the most capped player (140) in the history of English football

2015 England women finish third in the World Cup finals in Canada, their best ever performance

2016 Astonishingly, relegation favourites Leicester City, at initial odds of 5000-1, win the Premier League title

2017 Lewes FC becomes the first club in Britain to pay its women's team the same as its men's

2018 Manchester City break eleven top-flight records to win the Premier League title by a remarkable 19 points. England reach the semi-finals of the FIFA World Cup in Russia, eventually going down 2-1 to Croatia

2019 For the first time in the history of the English game two clubs end up with more than 90 points in the top flight. But only one can be Premier League champions. The England women's team wins the SheBelieves Cup in the USA and are one of the favourites for the FIFA Women's World Cup in France

CHAPTER 11

Playing 'Away' Is For Super Fans

SRC: By my way of thinking, the game is best preserved today through sacrifice and through conversation. You get a lot of both when it comes to serious away travellers. Only 204 fans might make the November trip, say, from Carlisle United to Grimsby Town, and they may not be specially feted by anyone for having done so (no one made them do it). But it is their noisy presence that is so invaluable for the integrity and survival of the game. The away contingent at smaller grounds is usually acknowledged by their hosts: the stadium announcer declares that 204 have made it, and thanks them for coming such a distance in such weather (he or she never accuses the opposition of a pathetic turnout, even if it is one). The visitors might enquire about what sort of 'library' this stadium is. The home fans, meanwhile, might break out into a mocking chorus of: 'You could have come in a taxi', knowing full well they probably won't send any greater number up to Carlisle for the reverse fixture.

JW: The Premier League has just started to cap away match ticket prices at £30. It's a cheap win and a clear recognition that away supporters provoke the core atmosphere at most matches. Their singing and gentle (and not so gentle) abuse keeps the home fans on their toes and buzzing. And it is the away end you hear loudest on TV when a 'great atmosphere' is being discussed.

SRC: The British atmosphere is what foreign broadcasters often talk about when they take the Premier League feed. It's part of what they pay for. They like the spontaneous, boisterous fan rivalries we have here as part of the TV package, something which money can't really buy elsewhere. In Italy and Spain you might get more fan choreography – mosaics and rehearsed performances – but here we like something a little more organic. For us, supporters are not the main show, but they can add plenty

Two policeman, helmets dislodged, try to control crowd disorder at the Spurs v Chelsea derby, White Hart Lane, April 1975
(Mirrorpix)

to the pleasures of being there.

JW: We know that some supporters value only travelling away these days. They have given up on home support because it feels so passive, so uninvolving. Watching away means standing up, really supporting and calling your club home in hostile territory. It can feel more like the old days, more confrontational. The best songs are also usually invented away and players notice you, sharing victories but also commiserations in defeat. Winning together in a 'difficult' place feels much sweeter than any home win. You also recognise people later, fellow supporters who you might have met in the most inaccessible and risky places with your club. I saw Liverpool play in St Petersburg against Zenit one icy and inhospitable February night, along with about 400 freezing Reds. All are devoted heroes in my book.

SRC: I love the criss-crossing of football supporter travel routes that goes on in Britain, particularly on winter

Saturdays. The service stations can be crazy places, as fans from all levels, travelling in all directions, briefly mix it up. 'Where are you going? We played there last week. Try the pies but look out for the stewards.' Mad places, too, are some key railway stations, like Crewe, truly a junction that almost every away football fan must have travelled through, or changed at, for an away trip at some point. Arriving at a destination railway station can be a challenge in itself: Where now? Follow the floodlights, follow the fans. For the FA Cup there might be a whole, Dunkirk-like, fleet of awayday match specials, tens of smart coaches followed by decrepit minibuses or weathered vans, usually filled with young guys whose drinking is monitored by older more experienced away travellers. Down the road they will be pulling up on a grass verge anyway, for a mass pee – or worse.

JW: Of course, some away fans will have to travel very much further than others, especially those in the far north, or the English south-west, or from South Wales. A BBC survey in 2018 showed that an especially dedicated Plymouth Argyle fan had travelled around 12,000 miles in a single season to follow the Pilgrims. Some supporters face travelling hundreds of miles just for home matches, regular 4 am starts. Their local away fixtures might feel more inviting than the home ones. These are the sacrifices we make for football. But we might have it rather easy here. After all, we are a relatively small nation with fairly decent transport routes. Consider this case: in March 2017, in the Russian second division, Luch-Energiya travelled to Baltika Kaliningrad for a league game. It was a single round trip made up of a cool 12,882 miles. I'm not sure how many away fans travelled, or if they felt the trip was really worth it – the match ended up a dire 0-0 draw. But we are back to the pleasures of suffering for football again, aren't we? I can still imagine a tiny band of Luch-Energiya fans exalting later over a beer about the 'terrible' nature of the trip, but the rewards of actually being there when what might prove to be a precious point was brought safely back home. Could it have been done without us? I don't think so.

SRC: Countries on that scale tend not to encourage much away support. And even here not all away fans are especially welcomed, though we're in the supposed post-hooligan era. Pretty much gone now are the days when large gangs of baggy-trousered, long-haired and booted-

'Millwall Are In Town' - Wolverhampton, 2015
(SRC)

up young 'lads' would parade up and down an unfamiliar high street, apparently looking for aggro. This show of visiting force – a gang mentality – wasn't always lawless. It could symbolise more of a Nat Lofthouse-style shoulder barge rather than a violent kick to the groin. But it looked impressive and its scale was often frightening to the afternoon shoppers. It also meant lots of running around and some welcome police overtime.

JW: The bark was often much worse than the bite. After Hillsborough, demand for away tickets began to change at the top level in England; different types of fans started to travel, women, lots more older supporters and mainly season ticket holders. But because of the forbidding reputation of some committed travelling fans, bars and pubs in distant places are not always that happy to see you arrive, even when you promise to behave yourself and drink the place dry.

The high street can be pretty segregated now, as well as the stadium. But regular away fans who travel in small groups in cars, can also devise their own checklist of 'quiet' pubs on the away schedule. There is far more contented mixing of rival football fans before matches these days than some people who don't know the game might imagine or admit.

SRC: For me, a lot of the attraction of travelling away can still be about family bonding, sometimes with just your dad, or with your dad, your brother and even your grandad. And plenty more women watch away games these days; as you say it's a more civilized experience in the away end. Maybe this is because we intrepid football

'A Couple Enjoy A Lock Out' - FC United at Colwyn Bay, 2011
(SRC)

travellers are treated less suspiciously in the ground now, less like dangerous, marauding prison escapees and a little more like customers whose money is as good as anyone else's and whose safety is paramount. A side-effect of this new friendliness is the mild disease of face-painting. It's part Braveheart and part creche at the local fete.

JW: I've always wondered what you do if you are fully painted-up but your team capitulates without a fight. Where do you go then? How long does the shame have to persist? Do you find a washroom right away, or just tough it out?

SRC: Down the leagues, fans of very small clubs don't bother with face painting. They have long enjoyed the gentler pleasures of away match travel, when you can be on first name terms with nearly everyone who goes. But the arrival on the non-league scene of FC United of Manchester in 2005 shook up some of that low-key attitude to visiting supporters.

JW: Some clubs cashed in and began to charge extortionate admission prices for these games. Others complained about the rowdy behaviour of some FCUM followers and wanted the club thrown out of the league. When the club joined the North West Counties League Division Two their opponents normally played before crowds of around 50 fans in total. FCUM produced an

average of 1,200 away supporters (and a dog), a real challenge and a complete change of climate.

SRC: How did FCUM fans solve the excess away support issue? Find a friendly hill, turn each occasion into a party, and hob-knob with 'the enemy', singing your hearts out, win, lose or draw. It seems to work.

JW: What happens if you move in the opposite direction, to away support for our national teams? The Scots and Welsh seem pretty comfortable in their own skins when they go abroad. But a curious thing seems to happen at international level for the English. Rather than fighting or quarrelling, as one might expect, the great urban tribes of England seem to naturally come together, briefly subordinating club allegiances in favour of patriotism for the national cause. But they don't entirely ditch their club identities – they bring them along for the ride. We get this complex merging of the national (the Cross of St. George) with the local (names of clubs, places and friends on the flags) in a giant expression of a fragmented, but united, national/local solidarity.

'Collective Responsibility'- England v France at Lisbon, 2004
(SRC)

It feels like a moment when all those smaller outposts of English club football can gather together. In fact, international tournaments increasingly rely on England fans turning up in their droves to make them a commercial and television success. The English have somehow become THE super away fans on the world stage.

CHAPTER 12

Saturday Afternoon, Sunday Morning

'Kirkbride The Captain Plays On' - Coniston, 1996
(SRC)

SRC: I wanted to try to say something through my photographs about village life, about the countryside and local football. This might sound quite straightforward, but it is actually surprisingly tricky. There's so much eulogising about the countryside today, it's as if the city is to blame for all life's ills. There is also a spate of nostalgia about the supposed authenticity of the grassroots game – as though professionalism in football threatened to kill the goose that laid the golden egg in a once leafier England all those years ago. We need to get over this.

JW: Grassroots football, especially outside big cities, for many people has come to signify something that is not yet spoiled, not gentrified. It is seen as green and pure, and with flourishing roots. In fact, some sports purists who may like football actually say that they prefer watching and playing the older game of cricket because they think cricket best reflects the gentle, pastoral elements of English village life. It is played by locals, often neatly

surrounded by a polite ring of supporters and volunteers, with (usually) female helpers making teas and scones. The vicar is probably next in the order to bat. This is John Major's vision of a bucolic England: the squire, cricket and warm beer. Football has a job competing with that.

SRC: Cricket, when you come across it after turning some corner into a village, *is* like a rather beautiful vision of England in white flannels. It even has its own soundtrack: the rarefied, hollowed out, slightly delayed, cracking sound of leather ball on willow. Some polite applause, birds tweeting. Cricket works a bit like the National Trust – like farmers preserving drystone walls – not so much to keep anything in or anyone out, but because it looks good to tourists and nostalgists.

JW: I think football works a bit differently in the countryside in that its role is partly to preserve the name and the standing of the village or small town; to keep together a group of lads (traditionally), a band of blood brothers, a cohort of young men almost awaiting a higher service. Which turned out to be the 'Greater Game' of war in the twentieth century. Local football teams – like war memorials – carry forth the names of places. They represent working men's identities in a way in which cricket, because of its perceived snobbiness (the Lord's Taverner's image), can sometimes find rather more difficult to do.

SRC: I have a village football tale to tell. I had recently arrived in the Lake District (where as it turned out I was to spend the next 28 years). I didn't have a local team and I thought a way to ingratiate myself with the local community was to roll up at the local club. Esthwaite Vale were not very good and had even folded and re-formed, but Coniston FC, they were legendary. So, over the fell I

'Versus Lunesdale Afore Skiddaw' - Braithwaite,1994
(SRC)

'Standing On The Corner' - Bolton Wanderers, 1995
(SRC)

ran with the farmer's pet dog who never got any exercise (I was lodging with his owners) and arrived in the pouring rain at the rickety bridge over a torrent of a stream beneath. Locals call this sort of heavy rain 'drizzle' and the water course a 'beck'.

Squinting through the rain splattering on the tin of the old changing-room, I could just about hear a few voices inside. So I knocked on the door and it fell silent within. Then suddenly the door flew open and the players were all sat sideways, or standing, stretching in various states of undress. The senior player nearest the door yelled at me: *"AND WHAT THE F*** DO YOU WANT?"*, then slammed the door shut. The soaking, shivering little dog looked up at me.

The door then opened slowly and they called me in. I got to train. To play. To be part of it. I swotted up on that legend of how, as a tough mining community (with a soft and gentle heart, of course) Coniston FC was certainly a club worth playing for. Fridays, spilling out of the Old Man (the mountain which gave everyone their living), the tin miners would race down the steep descent with their noisey steel-capped clogs, and into the village hall to find out if they were on Saturday's team sheet.

JW: It's no surprise that the emblems and badges of so many professional clubs carry reminders today of their roots in lost local industries: the Blades, the Irons, the Mariners. The connection between football clubs and local industries was pretty central right from the start.

SRC: For those selected for the Coniston team, who had already that day put in a hell of a shift down the mines, they could sit back and conserve their energy. Their next shift would be THE GAME. The reserves, however, could afford a drink or two and dance the evening away, promenading the local lasses into the night. Such was the close-knit nature of the community here, there were times when the entire first eleven was made up of just a few named families, the Walkers, the Kirkbrides, etc. To try to become more a part of this set-up, on more than one occasion I actually slept in the old main stand – I felt I had years and years of catching up to do.

JW: It can grab you like that, the appeal of the football club as a route into the heart of the local (male) community. Scots who had moved to north east towns and cities in England in the late nineteenth century often became members or shareholders in local football clubs to try to gain a foothold in urban civic life. It was the one way they felt they could demonstrate that they really belonged.

SRC: The photograph at Braithwaite (shown above), I took recounting my time in the Lake District league was even used as backdrop by Morrissey to one of his shows in Los Angeles. He was idealising the kind of rural English masculinity I myself had found so engaging at Coniston.

JW: I can see why the Bard of Salford might go for it. He has a weakness for that kind of cultural juxtaposition.

Carel Weight painting 'Village Cup Tie', 1946
(Courtesy of the owners, the PFA)

What I really like about this photograph – and I suspect Morrissey did too – is its essential informality and Englishness. In this country we play local football right down to the lowest level of organisation. If you have a set of shirts you can hire a pitch, register your club and play in a league. You need nothing else. These guys represent the very foundation of the English game, its roots deep down to neighbourhood and village level and silhouetted against those beautiful, rolling Cumbrian hills.

SRC: My photographs of rural football, always without crowds, stands or the spray-painted ultra green pitches of the professional game, tend to look a bit bleak because they are so earthy and simple. I wanted to capture in this particular photograph where the game came from. This is deepest Cumbria, but it also the story of the very history of the game in Britain. These guys really are like the dry-stone wallers of sport. They are playing to keep their villages alive, but also to preserve that vision of the English countryside we all expect to see.

JW: So it is rather like those idealised images of rural and town sports one can find in a few famous paintings. The artist LS Lowry, of course, rather brilliantly captured the historic relationship between working communities and football in northern English towns, those deep connections between industry, working class people and the game.

One of Lowry's sport paintings, *The Football Match*, sold for £5.6 million in 2011, a record for one of his paintings. It's probably a year's salary for even a moderate Premier League player today.

'Downhill From A Corner' - Heathwaite, Cumbria, 1997
(SRC)

'Continuing After The Match' - Edale, 2014
(SRC)

SRC: The Carel Weight painting on village football I have included here was completed just before *The Football Match*, so it comes from about the same period. It's from the collection owned by the Professional Footballers Association, based in Manchester. It has all the life and elements of the grassroots game, but we never see them on view in real life all at once, as you can do in a painting.

You can see here a serviceman edging onto the pitch. Perhaps he is returning from the war, or else waiting to be called up/selected? One of the women of the town is especially animated: dashing, poised, sprung, present. The goalie, in blood red, is punching the ball away, out of the frame and into the ether. Windswept trees and a dramatic sky suggest seasons passing and a real

sense of urgency. A church is bang in the middle of the painting, along with the game at the very heart of village life. A painting does not tell 'the truth', as we imagine a photograph does, but it can bring the defining elements of local life together, all in one scene.

JW: In 1999 the PFA bought at auction a very famous Lowry painting *Going to the Match*. It was about fans streaming to the Bolton Wanderers ground. I know it greatly inspired you – you wrote once that by your photography you wanted to show some of the detail missing in those extraordinary Lowry paintings. The PFA Chief Executive, Gordon Taylor, said that the painting captured: 'The heart and soul of the game, the anticipation of fans on their way to the match'.

SRC: I shivered in Lowry's footsteps taking this photograph of Burnden Park. His distant football supporters do feel as if they are an intrinsic part of the landscape. They are not extras or mere tourists. They clearly belong to this place; they even make it what it has become. They *are* the main subject.

JW: The reality in local football is that it is the collective that has to do everything to stage matches, something which is very important, I think. It is also a reminder that, not so long ago, young players had their own jobs to do inside professional clubs as part of their apprenticeships. They learned their trade by cleaning the boots of the senior pros, sweeping the terraces or painting the club stadium in the close season. There are fears today that some young elite players earn too much, have a sense of entitlement and have it all too easy. Too much, too young.

SRC: Most of my grassroots photographs have a focus on space, and I try to keep them very simple. People's roles in staging games are also made very clear. The players I encountered do have to pull their weight, or there's no game. They have to do things for the club in the 'hands-on' sort of way that younger professionals or Academy lads no longer have to do.

   The people in this vision of mine of local football are often shown working and muddied, obviously fully engaged. At Hathersage, I photographed a player in semi-darkness (the changing-room bulb had blown) having a shave ahead of playing in a match where very few people would be looking at him.

JW: Referees tend to be the forgotten men of the local game. They have no team to rally round and are often abused and left unconsidered. But without them local matches simply can't take place. Retired players can stay involved in the game by taking up the whistle, but it can be a tough gig. In 2017 Ryan Hampson, an 18-year-old local league referee from Manchester, called a reported 2000 local referees out on strike because of the way officials were being treated by both players and spectators.

SRC: In this photograph the referee, framed by peeling coloured walls, is taking a quiet moment at half-time to mop himself down for the second half. A few players have got in there first and cleaned their mucky boots on his main towel. Maybe this is a way of questioning the official's authority, away from the ball and without fear of a caution. The referee, alone with his own thoughts in the interval, is always in a very different place and mindset from the warming togetherness and chaos of the team dressing rooms.

JW: Playing for a local football club is still one of the main ways in which working class men – and increasingly women – make new friends when they move to a new town or city. No-one cares if you are the life of the party, or a quietly reserved type when you try out at a new club. They only want to know if you can play – the social niceties can come later. And football can also be a way of keeping up ties with the place you have left behind.

In London, where so many young people move for work, there are scores of teams playing in the very kits of the clubs supported back home. There is even a local league in which the fans of, say, Plymouth Argyle can regularly play those from Celtic, Manchester City and other famous names. This level of local football can be an excuse for a drink after the match or even for continuing where you may have left off the night before. Money is largely removed. There may be some 'expenses' paid to the star players, but mostly *they* pay to play and they are mindful of sorting out their own fines for bookings or for getting sent off. At this grassroots level you can hope for the odd local newspaper headline, but there are few media spats between players and managers, or discord between the fans and the team. There is a closeness for everyone present – even the officials might get a hot cup of tea now and then.

'Preparing For The Match' - Hathersage, 2015
(SRC)

SRC: So, there's you, from 'the village' or a small town maybe up north, someone who hates the game and all that village team niceness. And then you move to London, perhaps with a sense of relief or escape. But, lo and behold, you're soon dragged along to watch, or to be part of, the very thing you thought you had left behind!

JW: It can happen. And yet, for all this – for all the positive values local football can command – 11-a-side grassroots football tends to struggle to recruit today. Shorter versions of the game, played under lights on mid-week evenings, fit in better now with most people's busy lifestyles.

'Hope Valley League Ref' - **Stoney Middleton, 2014**
(SRC)

SRC: Things are changing, for sure. Ullswater United (back up there in The Lake District Westmorland League) can only keep going, can keep fielding a team from the valley now for over 100 years, by calling on 'mercenaries' from nearby Penrith. Someone fancies a season in the country, so he signs up. People who come to play will not necessarily share their trades anymore – if the clubhouse gets a leak, there is no longer a willing local plumber to call on.

Today's local teams are a bit divorced from the old line-ups that stare back at you in clubhouses, local pubs, home mantelpieces, or in the local library. But at the FA HQ at St Georges Park – which is about 180 miles from Ullswater – I had a chance encounter with one of the FA's marketing assistants. He told me that he dashes 'home' to Ullswater 'every once in a while' to keep goal for the club. I can appreciate anyone who wants to play for a village side, however irregularly. A warming story.

JW: Playing for your local place still means something. But as the traditional men's game goes downhill in its grassroots settings today, so there is one section of the football family that seems to be thriving. Local football for women and girls seems to be powering on...

CHAPTER 13

Women On The Side

'England Selfie' - St. George's Park, 2014
(SRC)

SRC: So, we have established that most young men want to do other things today rather than play local 11-a-side football on muddied fields. They want to be with their families, go fishing, watch sport on TV and so on.

Young women were never really encouraged to play sport at all. Then, about 100 years ago, they started playing football – and were good at it. This lasted about five or six years and then they didn't really play the game for another 50 years. But now they play again. It looks like they might be here to stay this time. Perhaps.

JW: That pretty much sums up matters. When the First World War broke out, British women from all kinds of backgrounds were ushered into munitions factories to do their patriotic duty. These women set up football clubs for leisure and to make money for the war effort and they drew large crowds to their matches. The Dick Kerr's Ladies from Preston were the stars, an early women's club that even went on international tours and represented England. After the war, the FA was concerned that the female game might obstruct men's football, so now the patriotic duty

of women was to give up work and football and return to their homes. When they refused, in 1921 the FA cooked up a charge that the funds raised in women's charity games were being misused. The upshot was that women were banned from playing at all grounds of FA registered clubs – which meant almost 50 years of potential development lost. Outcasts, a handful of women's clubs in England then went underground, until the 1960s when the England male World Cup win – and feminism – inspired a new generation of female players.

SRC: I can't help feeling that, throughout football's history in Britain, women have periodically scrambled out of the box with the ribbon on it, and then been put back in it. They have been used mainly to titillate the men's scene. The old male order, feeling threatened or something else, snaps the box shut. The 'meet the wife' mentality rules once more. 'Meet the husband' would be equally annoying and demeaning, of course, if the roles were ever reversed.

JW: Women in Britain have had to fight for the right to play from the very start. At least now most of the major men's clubs in England have developed and started to support women's teams. Manchester United were slow off the blocks for whatever reason – perhaps they were waiting to do it spectacularly in 2018 when it looked like they weren't going to do it at all.

SRC: So, there is a chance again for women in Britain to put their football boots back on. Whether or not they can get a foothold on the main pitch, remains to be seen. There are still very few towns or cities in the UK where the women's club is better known than the men's club. Women don't represent places in football in the same way as men's teams do, and thereby they don't claim

*July 1916, World War One - the stands of Tottenham Hotspur football ground have been
turned into a workshop, making gas masks helmets and other protective equipment for
the war effort. The work of women*
(Mirrorpix)

the ground. A few female clubs have shared stadia with the men, such as Chichester City Ladies FC but, mostly, women play elsewhere: at sports centres, local schools, in the park, or even out of town. The women's team at mighty Liverpool FC once had to be content with playing matches at the home of the Widnes Vikings, a rugby league club from outside the city. What a poke in the eye.

JW: Your photograph of the Manchester City player injured against Liverpool at the 'Home of the Vikings' could have been taken at any game, male or female. But notice there is no phalanx of doctors and trainers in attendance here; injury in the women's game is a lonely business. It also demonstrates beautifully the physicality

of women's football and the courage and resilience of female players after all those years when medical experts were regularly being wheeled out to tell us that women should not play sport at all because their bodies weren't up to it.

SRC: I never quite fathomed how I was always keen to flag up women's involvement in the male game, but initially I wasn't drawn to photographing women playing their own game. Then I realised why. It was because the women's game had no home; their clubs did not represent the town in a way that a men's club is seen as the club of the town. You never see graffiti about a women's club. Women had no football history, at least not one that we could easily

'One In The Eye For The Team' - Manchester City Women, 2014
(SRC)

*Woman (also on Page 226) reading the football laws,
by Szabados-Mavrák Norbert*

talk about. When women played, it was regarded as just an anomaly. It didn't matter who won, where they played and that there weren't any crowds to speak of. I've got over this now.

JW: The important thing is that women want their game to be considered on its own terms. They don't want it to be endlessly compared with the male game and there is no great push from female players to play alongside men. The top women in England have recently been professionalized in the Women's Super League, though their contracts are still tiny when compared to the top men. Given the more extensive TV coverage for women's football today I guess young girls now have some role models they can look up to. For the first time it is entirely possible for young girls in Britain to fantasise about having a career in women's football, which is a major step forward. Let's just hope that professionalism doesn't mean that some of the bad habits of the men's game intrude too much into the women's equivalent.

SRC: The artistry in the women's game, and how it has no cheating – okay, less cheating – than men's football has me as a convert. Maybe one day women will get their own homes and maybe they will represent the local town. There has been a recent defrosting here of the habit of keeping males and females apart, encouraged by the supreme power of the FA. Now, year on year, the FA raises the age when males and females can take to the same field – even if they are not quite all leaping into the hot tub together later. I also see more women officiating at both men and women's games in Britain. There are even some

women in power – or softish power – at the boardroom level of top male clubs. Karren Brady, chief executive at West Ham United, has a profile.

JW: I'm not sure Ms. Brady is everyone's choice as an ideal female role model in the game, but we do need more women in positions of influence, for sure. Why no top female coaches – why does the women's national team in England have a male coach? Did you know that 11 or the last 12 major international tournaments for women have been won by a female coach? Go figure.

Your photographs usually tell us that females in the male game in Britain have typically been confined to the kitchens or the backrooms, are poorly paid, and are not key decision makers. Some powerful men in football still seem to see women as little more than support workers or even childminders. In France in 2014, an ex-female player Corinne Diacre became the first woman to coach

'Mother And Son Man The Tea Bar' - Clydebank, 1995
(SRC)

a professional men's club. She now coaches the French women's national team, one of the strongest in the world. Could a woman manage a professional male club here – why not? We have a long way to go, though – that 50-year FA ban has really cost us.

SRC: British women have not been given an executive space in the football club car park because men think that they are the real drivers. Down the years, it has been presumed that most women don't really get the game. And certainly not the offside law. It was as if understanding that single law somehow defined who could become the footballing Doctor Who and who would become his (female) assistant. *Note: we now do have a female Doctor*

'Heading Practice' - City Of Football Campaign, Nottingham, 2016
(SRC)

on the BBC at last. A recent grassroots campaign, *This Girl Can*, run by Sport England was much more positive and was a runaway success – including encouraging girls to play football. I worked on the project in Nottingham. It has been winning new hearts and minds, as well as awards.

JW: Girls and their parents are much more assertive today about their right to play the game. No more pleading with the sport's authorities and no more acceptance of casual sexism seems to be slowly edging up football's agenda. The shirts worn by Cheltenham Ladies FC bearing the slogan – *No More Page Three* – are a brilliant and brave piece of sporting gender politics for the new century, don't you think? There is still some way to go, of course.

Elaine,19, had to nominate a goalscorer who would net her an additional £200 per goal for every goal scored in a certain period, 1973. She chose Pop Robson of West Ham
(Mirrorpix)

The LGBT community in Britain still gets a raw deal in football and there is no sign yet of a senior gay professional in the men's game who feels comfortable and secure enough to come out. England women's captain Casey Stoney showed the way in in 2014 when she spoke publicly about her female partner. Some fans – women as well as men – still see gender and sexuality

'Three Lionesses' - England Women, 2014
(SRC)

as battlegrounds on which traditional attitudes have to prevail at all cost. Things will change, but only eventually.

SRC: One of the most remarkable recent steps taken by any club in Britain aimed at levelling the gender playing field, has been at Lewes FC (est. 1885), who recently rebranded themselves as 'Equality FC.' Lewes is in a small, radical non-conformist pocket enclave of Sussex, just inland of Brighton, so you might expect something innovative here. In 2017 the local club introduced a policy of same pay for their men's and women's teams. They are also given equal access to the club's famous Dripping Pan ground. A smart marketing move – Lewes had loads of positive media coverage – but it may also be a statement about the future direction of travel for British football.

JW: Fair play to them. The women's game here seems to be in a really strong moment, demonstrated by your remarkable photograph of those three England international players. What determination and strength of character is revealed here. The looks on these players' faces say to me: 'We have been through stuff, but now you need to take us seriously because we are powerful and we are not going away.' I think we are all beginning to get that message at last. And if I had to place a bet on it, I would say that England's best chance of winning a World Cup or a Euro title in the near future definitely rests with women like these. And who could say that, after the struggles they have come through and the barriers they have faced they don't deserve it?

CHAPTER 14

The George, Best & Barney Effect

SRC: When George Best was in his pomp in the late-1960s and early '70s, routing the opposition single-handed on the football field by day and then going on an almost unbelievable dribble through the swinging sixties landscape of Manchester by night, he completely changed our ideas about football, celebrity and what it meant to be young. He was the best player I ever saw, for all kinds of reasons – and probably the first British footballer to act sexy and look truly young. Gone was the post-war monochrome era where you looked at photos of top players who already looked like old men. Those guys looked either too stiff, too pasty, or simply too old to play a thrilling, modern game. George turned all of that on its head, connecting rebellious youth culture to football.

JW: Changing times. George was electric and irresistible. But just a few years after Northern Ireland's tricky George emerged replete with his fashion, cars and girls, another significant footballing Best had also started the process of transforming the British game. His was a very different story.

Clyde Best was a Bermudan, and one of the first black players to resonate in the late sixties in England with young pretenders as well as antagonists. Clyde took some serious racist stick – even from his own 'supporters' at West Ham. 'I was like a fly in the milk' he would say later about being pretty much the only black footballer playing regularly in the English First Division, and an irritant to terrace traditionalists. But he bedded in and got his admirers.

SRC: He must have had real courage playing at that time, a lone black beacon. These days you might examine any major club that had no black players. Quiet Clyde B never complained about the terrible treatment he often received.

Clyde Best at Upton Park, March 1970
(Mirrorpix)

JW: It's true, black players were expected to take it all. Accepting racist abuse without complaint was often seen by their coaches and team mates as a kind of character test. He just had to suck it up, including even in the dressing room and on the training pitch. In August 1969, aged 18, Clyde was ready to take on Arsenal at Upton Park and a few weeks after this debut he scored his first West Ham goal (out of 47), against Halifax Town. Young black footballers in the UK can look back now at Clyde Best as one of the first guys to face racism inside the game and from opposing fans. British football supporters at the time seemed happy to purr and eulogize over famous international black players, such as Eusebio and Pele, but

Manchester United's George Best in the FA Cup fifth round match at
Northampton Town Feb 1970, which United won 8-2, with Best scoring six
(Mirrorpix)

these were black celebrities from over there. Back here it was a different story. Those fans who did want to oppose racism were even prevented by the FA and the Football League from launching their own campaigns to support black players. The authorities called this 'bringing politics into football.' Clyde simply soldiered on alone.

SRC: Two great football Bests, but living in different worlds. George, like Clyde, came from across the sea, albeit from nearby Belfast. He nearly returned there before his professional football career had really begun. George had his adventurous streak but, like Clyde, he was actually a shy boy – a lad tied to the Cregah estate. Had his early homesickness at Manchester United gotten the better of

him, we might have had a very different experience of the revolution he helped usher in. You could argue, I suppose, that George's celebrity lifestyle and TV image, in a way set out a marker for the global celebrity players who followed at Old Trafford, David Beckham and Cristiano Ronaldo. But, in the end, George found it just too much like hard work to keep his mad life on the rails. He was George Best on the pitch but for the tabloids and his drinking mates he was 'Bestie' off it.

JW: 'I was born with a great gift' George said, after his early retirement from the game, 'and sometimes with that comes a destructive streak. Just as I wanted to outdo everyone when I played, I had to outdo everyone when we

George Best with Miss United Kingdom, October 1966
(Mirrorpix)

were out on the town.' You did it, George. Early on, like lots of other players Bestie could get wrecked on a night out without it being splashed all over the news headlines. But when he started to miss training sessions that was harder to keep quiet. Later, in the age of saturation TV football coverage, social media and mobile phones, the game would become increasingly like a soap opera, with top players' social lives being endlessly picked over and exposed by the press, radio, TV and social media alike. Any real privacy or discretion for elite footballers in England is now pretty much over.

SRC: Don't you think Sky TV would have begged for a George Best, or a Gazza? Mind you, the drinking culture of English clubs has waned since George and Paul Gascoigne did their thing. New diets and a generation of foreign players and coaches have seen to that.

But the satellite companies have done pretty well out of the deals with the Premier League since 1992. In George's and Clyde's time, the modest TV income was split between all 92 Football League clubs. The newly minted TV rights money today is gobbled up by the top 20 and its players and agents, meaning today's footballers are uber-handsomely paid and a lot of them have a global

profile, not just UK domestic interest. Even George Best did not get rich playing football.

JW: The TV money has also brought in these foreign stars, blocking some 'home grown' talent. When only three-out-of-ten Premier League players is qualified to play for England you begin to wonder if the English club game has throttled the national team. But without Sky and BT Sport there is no way that British football could be quite so muscular globally and to manage to put its content way ahead of that from all other countries. No-one can question the commercial success of the Premier League and the power of its worldwide brand. Even British prime ministers hold it up as one of our great UK business success stories in the age of global deregulation. But at what cost?

By the mid-point in the season we now expect most managers in the bottom half of the Premier League will already have been sacked. We also expect some ambitious clubs in the Championship to spend much more than they can really afford to try to get promoted – and that some of them will crash and burn if they fail the test.

'Beckham And Scholes Before Him' - **England at Wembley, 1999**
(SRC)

SRC: It's like the song: *"You're just too good to be true, can't take my eyes of you – pardon the way that I stare, there's nothing else to compare"* (Frankie Valli as of The Four Seasons). Lots of people these days say about the Premier League: 'I don't really like it – the greed, the transfer fees and wage excesses' – but I just can't resist

'Barney's Footballing Pedigree' - **Berkhamsted Eagles, 1983**
The later Sky Sports guru clutches the match ball
(SRC)

it. Personally, I love it. I absolutely *love* it – like I love chocolate. But is it good for me, all this chocolate, and if I have too much of it will it make me feel just sickly?

JW: Chocaholic, you? I may be old fashioned, but I'm just saying that top football today is cash-driven and is a product made more for TV than for the people who attend matches or for local communities. Look at the interest today in VAR, ostensibly built to clear up 'obvious' mistakes made by match officials. People watching at the ground, inside the stadium, barely know what's happening when VAR is called up. 'Watch out for the ref holding his ear', that's all we get. We all know that VAR is really there to add value for TV viewers, football's new customers. Key people outside the game have shaped football's present format and will probably dictate its future.

SRC: It's men like Vic Wakeling and Barney Francis at Sky Sports we're talking about here, the men who pushed the current game well beyond the horizons of old school club directors and the grassroots heartland.

In an indirect and roundabout way, my own family may have played a small hand in this. Back in the early 1980s my brother founded Berkhamsted Eagles FC. These boys had *nirvana* in local football terms: rarely scraping for kit and funds, a flotilla of doting parents offering transport to away matches, Mars bars at half time and a rich social calendar off the pitch. The captain of one of these Eagles' sides became Sky Sports' guru Barney Francis, the man who in 2016 shook hands with the Premier League executive on a TV deal worth a mind-numbing £5.14 billion. Small world, eh?

CHAPTER 15

The Big Match Of The Day

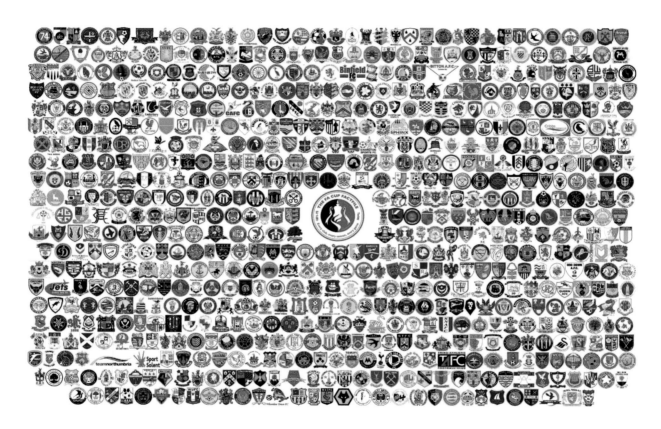

The entire array of FA Cup entrants 2018-19,
prior to the Preliminary Rounds which start in August
(Courtesy of @FACupFactFile)

SRC: Even in this amazing new Premier League era when live TV football rules, we still have, tiptoeing through this period, BBC's *Match of the Day*. The choice match highlights of the day. This was the way we all used to receive the game on TV – extended highlights of selected games, covered by the BBC and also delivered in *The Big Match* show on ITV.

JW: They are showing repeats of The Big Match now on BT. Three things strike you right away: the terrible state of the pitches in the 1980s; how slow and unathletic the game seems compared to today's quickfire, skill-rich football; and the fact that those old football TV programmes were not dominated by repeat appearances of a handful of big clubs.

The entire array of Scottish Cup entrants 2018-19,
prior to the Preliminary Rounds which start in August
(Courtesy of @FACupFactFile)

SRC: Today, when the BBC or ITV covers an FA Cup game live – they still get very large audiences, even if smaller clubs are involved. Because somehow it is the national community watching football again, wanting a David and Goliath chapter from the football bible. It is not just those people who are star-gazing and who can afford to have satellite subscriptions.

JW: I think that's an important point. Watching football on TV was once, somehow, a communal demonstration of what you shared with other people, a kind of civic ritual as a citizen, rather than a signal about whether you were able to afford to buy access to the game, watched with a select few.

SRC: In 2018, you can watch live pretty much any match you like now on TV. It's all about choice – if you have the money. But choosing too much processed food will soon do you in. And the single most popular football programme on TV is still *Match of the Day*, even though it is on at an awkward time and you can often be falling asleep on a Saturday night trying to stay up to watch it. The wholesome Gary Lineker still hosts. On *Match of the Day* the message always seems to be: you should watch this, because this is really *good* for you.

JW: It is officially the longest running football TV programme in the world. *MOTD* began in 1964 in black-and-white and it has managed to hold its place in the schedules regularly ever since, because people negotiating the TV deals for the Premier League realised that they also need access to the national audience for football, to try to keep the game alive in every household.

SRC: The really big 'live' football TV moments of my childhood were usually around the FA Cup because, for me, the cup was a tale about the nation. It was like the Grand National of football. Everybody could enter and

*Destination Wembley. Fulham supporters on the way to see their team
take part in THE game of the season, the 1975 FA Cup final*
(Mirrorpix)

then the last two clubs left standing made it to the final at Wembley and everyone sat in front of the telly and applauded them. It felt like the whole country stopped to watch the FA Cup final at 3pm on a Saturday afternoon in May. It ended the football season and waved in the cricketers. The FA Cup always represented the gallant side of the game, with great sportsmanship, excited kids in the crowd, giant-killings, and players politely applauding their opponents off the pitch.

JW: The oldest cup competition in the world, and it can still thrill today. The FA Cup was the first really national competition in England, because the Football League was initially dominated by clubs from the north and midlands.

So, winning the cup became a focal point for many clubs and a welcome counter to the marathon slog required in the league. It took Liverpool FC 73 years to win it. However, top clubs use the FA Cup today to rest players for the greater struggles ahead: for the Champions League or staying in the Premier League, where the big money is.

SRC: Since the FA Cup has become 'devalued', I really think there may be a case for saying now that all clubs should enter at the same stage – the first week of August, just after the round of summer friendlies – and see who gets to Wembley in May.

Who knows, the giants could meet preposterously small football clubs before they have even properly

SRC: And another thing: Wembley Stadium should always be owned by the English game as well as being used for the FA Cup final only. I don't want it to end up being a home for American Football.

JW: I understand your fears about selling off our best silver but you have to show a little flexibility. Holding the Football League play-offs and the various trophy matches at Wembley has really democratised the place, and has given lots of fans of smaller clubs a fantastic experience. Doesn't every football fan, no matter their level, deserve at least one day in the sun as invited guests?

The Graf Zeppelin passing low over Wembley Stadium during the FA Cup Final of 1930 in which Arsenal beat Huddersfield Town. The airship, longer than the pitch, was booed by some of the crowd who thought it an uninvited distraction
(Mirrorpix)

awoken to the new season. They could be giant-slayed on a sloping ground – or one where the corner is higher than the height of the goal crossbar (as at Heathwaite FC's pitch besides Lake Windermere). What fun! So British!

JW: I admire your romance and ambition, but the bigger clubs would cry foul very loudly about this crazy idea. They complain already that they play too many matches, and having Premier League clubs at really small grounds in August would be a security nightmare. We would also lose the aura of the third round, always the first week in the new year, when the big boys get thrown in and the surviving minnows start to dream. The FA Cup seems likely now to become a mid-week, no replay, competition. More history lost. But we should stop hawking the TV rights to the draw to the highest bidder. Can't we get back to making sure that everyone has at least *played* before the next round draw is made?

CHAPTER 16

The Show Must Go On

Valley Parade fire, Bradford City, May 1985
- sweeping through the mainstand in the 5 minutes before half-time
(Mirrorpix)

Old Trafford suffers a direct hit, March 1941 - the most extensive damage
suffered by any league club during the war
(Mirrorpix)

JW: Historically, the game in Britain has been very slow moving, we both know that. Clubs don't like change, fans don't like change. Most of the disasters in British football have actually come about because the game has refused to modernise, has been idle in looking to the future and in caring properly for its supporters. And yet, these are also some of the moments when British football has been forced to gather itself and change quite radically. This applies especially following that sequence of terrible tragedies that hit the British game in the 1980s, including the horrific fire in the Bradford City stadium in 1985.

SRC: The tough, rough 1980s with a series of fatal disasters were heartbreaking, I for one started to care deeply about the game. But I would concede that the game in this country has always been subject to interruption, going right back to the start. Two world wars – you can't get bigger interruptions than that. Football in Britain has often been faced with having to pick itself up and start again. Bramall Lane – home for football and cricket – was bombed, so Sheffield United had to play at Hillsborough. Old Trafford was bombed and Manchester United played at Maine Road. Ironically, in February 1985 a match was postponed at Bramall Lane because an unexploded German bomb was found nearby.

JW: In the initial stages of the First World War, the game's authorities in Britain refused to follow the lead of the amateur Rugby Football Union to stop playing matches. The administrators in football argued that it was better to keep professional leagues going to maintain the morale of the people back home. 'It will all be over by Christmas' sort of thing. This was a very reasonable position to take but, of course, footballers and football people were criticised in the national press for being unpatriotic. While public school educated army officers were kicking and chasing a football into some muddied deathtrap of a no man's land in France, working class professional football players were lording it in safety back home. This was the story. A lot of it was simple class prejudice. Eventually the football authorities gave in.

SRC: During the Second World War, players and fans were scattered all over the place. Turning up at grounds and makeshift matches they could never have imagined a few years before. There were plenty of players guesting at other clubs, depending on where they were based in the forces, so there was some continuity there. A little bit of pleasure in these extraordinary times. But these elongated interruptions must have been dulling and totally debilitating and were very different from the other thing that we really love contending with in Britain, and that's the weather. That's all part of it, football's winter tale. Try to get your pitch fit, whatever the skies throw at you.

JW: A lot of great British footballers lost the key years of their career because of war and, inevitably, a number of them did not come home. The 17th (Service) Battalion, Middlesex Regiment was formed as a Pals battalion during the Great War, with a core group of professional footballers – the Footballer's Battalion. The Liverpool and England international Tom Cooper died serving for the Royal Military Police in 1940.

Liverpool v Spurs at Anfield, April 1968. Bob Paisley carries off his injured skipper, Emlyn Hughes
(Mirrorpix)

SRC: Romantics, such as me, like to think that when league football finally resumed after the interruption of war, with all that horrible death and destruction, football was THE place to get folk back together again: a cheapish thrill. All that singing and supporting, shoulder to shoulder, without a real enemy. Is that why football in Britain was so popular in the late 1940s? People putting damaged lives and communities back together. These turned out to be the peak years through the turnstiles: the highest attendances ever across the country. Football crowds in Britain then eased off in the 1950s and 1960s, presumably because people found other things to do, the consumer society and all that.

Gravesend & Northfleet prepare for Sunderland in the FA Cup, February 1963
(Mirrorpix)

JW: Football was so popular immediately after the Second World War war because there really wasn't very much for working class people to do in Britain. Football, the pub, the dance hall and the pictures was basically it. Some cities were really badly damaged by bombing and going to the game for men offered both an escape from the privations of the war years and a comforting return to some kind of normality. As Britain slowly recovered and wages for working people improved, so some fans did find other interests around new forms of consumption – DIY, home leisure, family outings, sport on television. Some younger supporters also began making a nuisance of themselves at the match. The local football club was no longer the automatic Saturday afternoon outing for respectable working men and their mates. Wives and girlfriends wanted some leisure time too.

SRC: It was a place where men, particularly, could become embedded, lose themselves. The mantra that 'The show must go on' is always around in football and it's quite a blokey thing of rolling up the sleeves and jumping into the cockpit of a digger that goes 'rat-tat-tat'. 'We must mend the pipes today' or 'Fix the floodlights.' No matter the state of the ground, the snow or the floods, the view of the office staff and the groundsman is always: 'We'll get this game on!' Even Bill Shankly learned how to shovel snow. For the trainer, the spongeman, it's: 'Get the injured guy off the field, however we can do it, and then get him back on.'

I think solving national problems begins with the kind of resilience shown in small incidents in sport at the local level.

JW: Fair point. But post-war players were not really that well looked after in this respect. Photographs of players being carried off on the back of trainers also tells us something about the condition of British football. Few clubs had qualified medical staff and players often feared the treatment table. Before substitutes were allowed in league football in Britain (1965), injured men were usually made to return to the fray in order to add nuisance value, even if they could barely walk. Bert Trautmann broke his neck in the 1956 FA Cup final and played on. In the 1965 final – just before substitutes were allowed – the Liverpool defender Gerry Byrne broke his collarbone early in the game, but he kept his counsel and played on. Both City and Liverpool won.

SRC: Players were hard nuts in those days. So, the biggest off-field interruptions were the two wars, weather, and I guess you could also say the recession in the 1930s had an effect. But I know I'm right in saying, that something which also had a huge impact on attendances later on, was the Heysel disaster in 1985 and then what happened at Hillsborough.

Bill Shankly helps clear Anfield, Christmas 1964
(Mirrorpix)

JW: Heysel more than Hillsborough, I think. Heysel was definitely the lowest post-war point in English football in terms of image, public reactions to the sport and falling crowds. Aggregate league attendances in 1948/49 were over 41 million; the season after Heysel they were down to just 16.5 million, and the game was also weighed down by some terrible newspaper headlines. I think a lot of people just gave up on English football at that point, had had enough of the fan violence and the awful facilities.

But modernisation had already begun. The play-offs were introduced in England in 1986/87, signalling a greater understanding that most people now expected more than simply watching their local club playing out relatively meaningless end-of-season fixtures. The play-offs helped make football matter to more fans and to a new generation of supporters. By the time Hillsborough happened, football crowds in England were already on the rise again. The show was slowly getting back on the road.

SRC: The Taylor report, after Hillsborough, was also important here because Lord Justice Taylor basically talked about who we are as a people, why football was important to us. He discussed what we, the nation, wanted – and had a right to expect – from the game. He helped map out a new road to recovery.

JW: Lord Justice Taylor knew that the government at that time didn't really care about football or about the people who watched it. To these politicians, football in England

The Day After Xmas Encounter' - Sheffield Wednesday, 1990
(SRC)

was just an embarrassment, a repeating policy problem. But Taylor listened to fans and wondered aloud why the sport was being so badly managed and why supporters who cared so much about the game were not being treated like customers – a dirty word to a lot of fans.

Taylor at least understood something about why football mattered so much to so many people and that it needed a radical shift to thrive. He wanted better and safer facilties (which he saw as seats) and a better general treatment for supporters, but also a change in attitudes. He was trying to drag the game, kicking and screaming, towards the 21st century. His report, plus the entrepreneurial ambitions of the men who wanted to lead football post-Hillsborough, plus the economic problems of satellite TV, all coalesced in the early 1990s.

And out popped the Premier League in 1992!

SRC: A whole new ball game, no less. The other way we get the message, loud and clear from British football, that 'The show must go on' is when we think about how few clubs have actually been allowed to completely disappear, no matter the disasters, their financial problems or their low levels of active support.

There is a real sense in the British game that, come what may, the local football club must somehow survive. Very few clubs in this country have bowed out completely. They are constantly being resurrected, with supporters' groups or local investors breathing dear life into their corpses. In a strange way, it seems that if your football club goes under then the place where you live somehow disappears with it. If war cannot destroy clubs then nothing else can.

CHAPTER 17

Football As Brand

SRC: So the Taylor report offered a new direction for British football. But how did clubs respond to those big 'interruptions' we discussed in Chapter 16, especially the recent toll of tragedies? English football seemed to develop a new three-sided balance in the 1990s, between acknowledging fans as consumers (and so ensuring they got better treatment and more safety), promoting the glossy brand of Premier League football at the top, but also trying to hold on to a sense of football's great heritage as the authentic side of this equation. So the game is in this triangular balance now: consumer-brand-heritage. It means that all clubs should be able to hold on to the authentic element of their appeal and that smaller clubs have just about enough money coming in. But the game also recognises that football, at some level, has to be a business. The new divisions feel more like a case of Skint v Loaded.

JW: I think it is true that while some clubs really struggle financially, the game at the top level is trying hard to balance its business interests with sporting ones. Fans believe too often business wins out. But what constitutes 'authenticity' today is often very contentious for football supporters.

SRC: For fans at some clubs, coming out with a string of expletives, or having a proper row with rival supporters at a match, might be perfectly 'authentic' for them. My photograph of a wreck of a terrace at a Brighton v Millwall play-off match at the old Goldstone Ground in 1991 sums this up.

There is a bit of a rivalry between these clubs and you might ask: where is all the crowd? Have they all gone home? In fact, the game is raging on somewhere below, out of sight. This young boy is being helped out through the broken pieces of a closed terrace by a first aid man.

It looks like the supporter has been hit on the head by a brick or something.

To get the fan to somewhere safe, he has to be taken through what might, metaphorically, be regarded as English football's decaying past. It's meant to be a symbolic picture about the game on the edge of big changes. It is about where English football is trying to get to and the awkward steps it might still have to take to get there. And there may also be some displacement of the 'old guard' coming at this very moment, either because standing areas of grounds were being closed down – like here – or because clubs just didn't want certain type of supporter anymore.

JW: This is a sharp reminder of aspects of 'the bad old days' and that safety would soon come high up on English football's new agenda. Fans at different clubs certainly do have their own ideas about what constitutes 'authenticity' and the club 'brand' – which is likely to be quite different from how most club owners see it. The songs that supporters sometimes sing about themselves, and about how fans of other clubs see them, is authentic for them, a key part of their identity. So, there can be a big difference between the official packaging of football today and how local people on the terraces and in the stands respond to the game. This can easily put some supporters at odds with the clubs they love. They might think that their own chief executive focuses far too much on the corporates, merchandise and the store – but that is part of the new equation that you were just talking about.

SRC: The Goldstone Ground had seen better days, but the new Brighton stadium, the Amex, does feel to me like it's part of the community and that the club has opened itself up to all sorts of inclusive activity and support for local fan initiatives.

'Led Away Hurt' - **Brighton & Hove Albion, 1991**
(SRC)

JW: I know Brighton fans have been involved in progressive pro-LGBT campaigns which have been largely supported by the club. This might smack of 'new' football for some traditional fans but it is important. Brighton's story of being displaced, homeless, and then returning to the local area as a successful and responsible Premier League club in a very smart stadium is also an inspiring football tale for today.

SRC: How does authenticity work in a two club city? Sheffield United and Sheffield Wednesday fans might have some minor differences about branding and what is authentic for them. Fans of both clubs might welcome investment from abroad, because it gives their club more chance of getting promoted and of getting one over on their local rivals. But on the day when these clubs meet the song that will be booming out loudest from Sheffield United fans will be a very local one, which has a very local meaning, about 'a greasy chip butty.' These United fans have adapted a conventionally romantic ballad and made it a powerful and moving football anthem, but one that is only remotely romantic and meaningful to the supporters who sing it. And me.

JW: The point is, it almost doesn't matter what is happening, business-wise, to clubs like these when they meet. Whether one club has more global ambitions, or one has gone down the foreign investment route more than the other. The core meaning of that match to those supporters will be pretty much the same as it's always been. There is a kind of 'essence' of Sheffield United, which will always be playing an 'essence' of Sheffield Wednesday; a meeting full of all those memories of past encounters and how these two clubs identify in the city. 'Hark now hear the Wednesday sing' will be coming from the other side. Everything has changed, but everything also remains the same. People who are less connected to Sheffield, who may be watching this match on TV in distant parts of the world, will have a very different take on it, of course. They might ask out loud: 'I wonder where Sheffield is?' For them, it might just be another blue-and-white stripes versus red-and-white-stripes. After all, until recently, global football fans even wondered where exactly Leicester City were based.

'Gingerbread On The Street' - Sheffield Wednesday v Sheffield United, 2012
(SRC)

SRC: Footballers from the past were brands in a sense, but very small brands. They often had to find another income. They ran a pub perhaps. Possibly not in the town where they made their name – and so the pub becomes a bit of a tourist attraction. Then players became bigger brands. In the internet age, someone like David Beckham became much less known for his heroic sporting character than for his commercial ambitions and his media-friendly

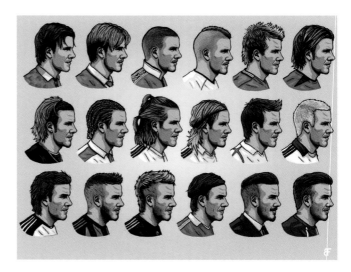

The changing hairstyles of David Beckham.
(Courtesy of Ben Farr Illustration)

personality. Beckham became a global icon, someone whose image was no longer 'contained' by football, by Manchester United or by the Premier League itself. His haircuts were also monitored pretty much on a daily basis at one point. He became an industry in his own right – a cultural brand recognized all over the world, and not just because of football.

Some clubs such as Leeds United, have a brand image that can somehow support as many as eleven different matchday scarves, expressing an unbelievable range of things that just don't seem to add up.

JW: I think this is a great photograph because it demonstrates so well both the enduring inventiveness and humour of football culture – though it's not always *that* funny – but also the new patterns of consumption developing around the game in the Premier League era. There are just so many potential football identities in play now, we are clearly beyond the age of, simply, following your local club and wearing its standard colours.

The game is so tied up today with the marketplace, with matters of consumption and catering for different styles of support and with offering choice about how you demonstrate your fandom. Working out how to access different fan constituencies is all part of increasing the appeal of the product. It is a message, I'm afraid, about how football is increasingly packaged, just like any other brand or cultural activity, to maximise its customer impact.

'Carrying The English Beckham Baby'
England v Brazil at Shizuoka, Japan, 2002
(SRC)

'To Decorate One's Self' - **Leeds United, 2012**
(SRC)

SRC: You could say that this sort of thing has kind of dissipated the one central push of what it means to be a fan of any club – or you could say it's expanded it. You can click on any of these channels and they will all bring you Leeds United, but each in a slightly different register.

JW: True. But once you get inside the stadium among your fellow Leeds supporters, then most people are still doing pretty much what they have always done: getting behind the club and experiencing that powerful and anonymising sense of collective solidarity. Football, rather cleverly, still offers the traditional attraction of being involved in something much bigger than the individual – all in one community – but it has also responded to the individualizing impact and appeal of wider social changes. You can choose how you, as an individual, want to be seen to be a fan, while also blending into the home support when you want to feel a part of the crowd.

SRC: Standing out at football still seems important to some people. Most British football supporters will probably have an aversion to my photograph of this pair of England-Beckham supporters in Japan in 2002. It may be more offensive in a way, than the photograph of all those Leeds scarves. At international level, it's almost as if football can say that we can market the game in any way we like because there are more than 200 countries out there and they all have different tastes. The Russians,

hosts to World Cup 2018, and others may not like this 'English' style of 'family' supporting, but the Japanese do – they get 'Kitty cute'.

JW: All the photographs in this chapter, taken together, tell us that there are so many different versions of iconic stars out there, so many brand options, and so many different ways of being a fan today, that you can connect with football in pretty much whatever way you like. Perhaps we need to be a little more tolerant of people who want to express their support for the game in these different ways, rather than laying down any hard-and-fast rules about 'authenticity' or what a 'real' fan looks like. We know that some fans will never be able to attend a match of the club they support, and that the global reach of the very large clubs in England can be tailored so that this doesn't impact too much on local fans.

All fans matter irrespective of the scarf they choose, or the baby they hold. Despite everything in the UK from 2016 onwards – including the Brexit we now face in 2019 – the football brand seems to ride out the major storms buffeting Britain. It is a brand that stretches across different Leagues, geographies and financial inequalities within the UK, where devotion and attendance hold true. It is the baby. It is the real McCoy. Even in the USA, home of baseball the NBA and the NFL and where TV invariably appears to be a better way of receiving 'live' sport, soccer attendances are soaring.

CHAPTER 18

The Attendance Is Important

JW: In Britain, nothing in football can replace the thrill of being there. How could it? This British obsession with football attendance goes right back to the early years of the game. Aston Villa were getting crowds of 40,000 in 1903. Nottingham Forest could only attract 1,500 for the visit of Stoke City. Remember that 200,000-plus crowd that hustled into the first Wembley FA Cup final way back in 1923? And what about the 147,365 who were officially present for the 1937 Scottish Cup Final between Celtic and Aberdeen at Hampden Park? Plenty more sneaked in. I think only the Brazilians and maybe the Portuguese, historically, come close to these sorts of figures. And even today the second tier, the Championship in England, draws higher aggregate attendances than the top leagues in France, Italy and Spain. We truly love *going* to football here.

'The Gasheads Gaskets Tested' - Bristol Rovers at Wycombe Wanderers, 2014
(SRC)

SRC: Attendance can be as important to some football fans as the score. We always ask: How many came? Was the ground full? Did little Matlock Town get a crowd?

For all the pressures from the Sky and BT paymasters and for all the top-level focus on the global footprint of the Premier League, we all want some validation, to experience something special, by being able to say: 'I was there.' But how do we value attendance? Should a smaller Football League club be convinced that the drip-down payment (from Barney's Premier League TV deal) compensates for a home crowd of, say, 3,000 when they had budgeted on home matches bringing in 4,500-plus? But this is no real measure compared to the wider value of football at smaller clubs. Is an entire season at Grimsby, for example, with all the marvellous images and experiences it conjures up, really worth less than a lower end Matisse painting? I don't think so.

JW: I hadn't expected that fine art comparison. Let me try a different tack, to make a similar point. I read a story recently about a fan called Kitty Thorne, from Trowbridge, Wiltshire. Kitty used to head off on the midday steam train to the old Bristol Rovers ground with a packed lunch of corned beef sandwiches and a flask of tea to watch her club play. Her first match was in 1954 when she was close to 40, and she was still attending in 2018 at 103 years of age. How many honours did Rovers win in those 64 years? I can tell you that: a couple of play-off wins and a Third Division title in 1990. Kitty only had to wait 36 years for it. She was not going for the glory, that's for sure, something else kept her motivated. She was a bit like so-called 'super fan' Pete Moran.

Since 10th November 1987 – when Ronald Reagan was US president and Tiffany's 'I Think We're Alone Now' topped the UK pop charts – Pete has been to every one of Stoke City's matches, home or away. Just think about that for a second: illness, family events, holidays, weather, transport issues. Nothing stopped him getting to Stoke games.

'The Attendance Is In' - Matlock Town, 2014
(SRC)

SRC: Sometimes, you just have to admire – and maybe be slightly concerned about – the utter devotion of some supporters, no matter their age or the stature of the club they follow. The compulsion of attending matches shows that the game is much more than a mere hobby or entertainment. It gets in your blood.

JW: That's because for football supporters always 'being there' often re-states something important about our identities and our place and family ties; about our loyalty to friends and to our club. But I think it can also say something about a collector's fetish and a deep-seated fear: What if something truly amazing happens and I'm not there? Those groundhoppers and people who never miss a game always seem to be men of a certain age. Some people deride them as train-spotters – as anoraks.

SRC: Forget the turnstile cash – football means little to a TV audience if the ground isn't full, or close to it. 'Why should I bother watching on TV if this club has no fans of its own?' For me, someone who photographs ordinary football people and who sees their value as part of the fabric of the sport, seeing massed banks of fans also says something about our values as a nation. I hope my photographs of fans add some value to football, reinforcing the message about why supporters who go to matches matter so much to the game.

JW: I remember that the AC Milan owner, Silvio Berlusconi, once said that if fans stopped attending because too much football was being shown on TV, clubs should pay them to come – as one might pay extras in a television spectacular.

'Show Of Colour' - Leicester City, 2013
(SRC)

Fortunately, we still appreciate our football clubs, not just for what they have achieved or how much money they are worth, or even the TV audiences they may get in China. We still look at how many people actually want to pay to watch them play. How many people express that irreducible commitment to the cause?

Look, we simply don't have that many public events these days where people from very different backgrounds and social classes can still sit or stand together and really share something significant in their lives as they do at football. Nobody in Britain thinks that a club such as Newcastle United, for example, is not important just because it has not had much recent success. We look instead at its history and the current attendance figures and marvel at north-east supporter loyalty and their belief that, one day, all this may change. We all know how important cases like Newcastle United are to the wider football narrative. And we all know how that club's supporters feel in their quarrels with owners.

SRC: And my quarrel with gallery curators was that they told me that football had no place in art galleries. I said 'We shall see'. My show went on tour for an unbroken span of 15 years – all at publicly funded art galleries. Is there anything as operatic and strangely beautiful as seeing a decked-out 50,000 strong football crowd sing its favourite anthem. The longest-running plays eventually come and go, but football never goes: it just keeps on running. Football grounds are not usually officially listed for public protection, but virtually every football ground is revered in the sporting public's psyche. Our historic football grounds don't need a blue plaque to be valued by the fans who fill them.

JW: It is interesting that there are groups of football supporters in this country – usually middle-aged men – who like to visit the most obscure football places, to be present in some of the smallest football crowds, because they are collectors and they appreciate the quirkiness and the diversity of the live football experience. You can visit significant and attractive places in England, Scotland, Wales and Northern Ireland by attending football. Some fans even write lyrical top-selling books about the camaraderie and the adventures in the game's lower reaches. Some supporters might insist on boasting about having 'been there' at some of the sport's biggest ever fixtures – about half-a-million Englishmen claim to have been at Wembley on 30th July 1966 – but there are plenty more who will happily bend your ear in a pub about being among the 346 souls who travelled to Derbyshire in heavy drizzle for a mid-table non-league contest in an open field that barely drew a line of national press coverage.

SRC: I worry that this might be a specifically British male mentality; something that goes right back to ideas of drawbridge Britain, and 'the island' and sacred ground, and that 'No other should tread on this land than us.' At some moments I think it might be all that sort of inward-looking stuff that is going on here. And then I change my mind and think: what a wonderful way of wasting one's time, if that is indeed what it is.

JW: Consider this: in March 2019 Wrexham FC, exiles in the fifth tier of the English game – the fifth tier, mind – drew a crowd of 7,106 to watch the home National League match versus Chesterfield. And even this was dwarfed by the 8,283 people who turned up on Boxing Day to see the Welshmen hammer Salford City. Ligue 1 club and Champions League regulars AS Monaco in France often have smaller crowds! What a quite remarkable people we are for attending football at all levels.

CHAPTER 19

Foxes At 5000-1

SRC: We could have called this final chapter: 'In Extra-Time' or 'The Fat Lady Sings'. We all know that in every season, and possibly every week, English football throws up wonderful stories. Blackpool; Huddersfield Town; Hull City; little homespun Barnsley, all at one time in the Premier League. Pull the other one! And then cue the street celebrations. And what about Burnley's return from disappearing up the Colne Valley? These are all great short stories in their own right.

But Leicester City actually winning the Premier League title in 2016 – well, that's a complete volume of fairy tales right there.

JW: I live in Leicester and my family are all City fans. We had journalists from all over the world descend on the place in 2016. The whole city was caught up in the narrative of that title season, wondering when the dream was ever going to end. To everyone's astonishment, it didn't.

SRC: We will get back to Leicester City later, but first can I mention an entire exhibition I made about just one game. We called it: May 13th 2012. Manchester City gave me special access that day. They just rang me up and said: 'Please come along and capture what will hopefully be our happiest day for a long time.'

They were not bragging, or taking things for granted, but they wanted a record of what happened. All the gallows humour of the previous 20 years at Manchester City hovered over the stadium that afternoon.

City had to win against lowly QPR to secure the club's first title for 44 years but, typical City…

The match didn't go to plan! The City fans were helpless, looking at their kids' faces for reassurance. No-one knew quite what to do, the very life was draining out of them. And, worst of all, it was the club down the road,

'Bottoms Up' - Barnsley, 1997
(SRC)

Manchester United, that was going to gain from this most colossal of all cock-ups.

I got myself between the City and QPR fans to capture both sets of fans' emotions, but I somehow knew I had to get to the end that City were attacking for the final few moments, even though it looked a lost cause. Call it a photographer's instinct.

Then, Edin Dzeko scores a header and, with pandemonium breaking out all around, the great man Aguero slides in the winner. BOOM! I think I can even divide my work in football by that day – BC (Before City) and afterwards – because the experience on that one afternoon in Manchester just fried me and served me up all over again.

And, football, being football, you think you have really seen it all now, that there will never be another day quite like this one. I really should have known better. Just four years later Leicester City took it to another level. They provided an answer to all those doubters and moaners in the pub who say that the game is 'Just about money'.

JW: Approaching the run-in in 2016. I think everyone in Leicester knew that this was a once in a lifetime opportunity for this club. The bookmakers certainly did: they had initially offered odds of 5000/1. You could get a better price on finding intelligent life on another planet. My own mother-in-law is a Leicester season ticket holder in her eighties and I think she knew that her decades of loyal support and longing had been building up to this one, tantalizing moment. Four lost FA Cup finals, no league titles. Could the Foxes really hold it together at the last, hold their nerve?

Every conversation with non-fans in Leicester towards the end of the season seemed to begin: 'I don't normally like football, but…' The entire city was gripped, people from all sorts of ethnic and cultural corners felt involved. I think only football can do this, can bring people from all kinds of social backgrounds inside the community tent in a mass celebration of who we are. It can reach beyond the market and community boundaries. It still matters to people.

There was something indefinable – almost mystical – about *that* group of players, and *that* coach, and *that* crowd working in perfect harmony for a few months in Leicester. It reminded us all, I think, that in the twenty-first century, for all the money talk and ownership wrangles, for all the investment angles and the asset stripping

'Players Celebrating Promotion' - Leicester City, 2014
(SRC)

and the massive player salaries, this is still a glorious, unpredictable sport, not simply a business. A man such as Jamie Vardy could still rise from a career in non-league football and a period on an electronic tag to be at home among these international thoroughbreds and to win a Premier League title medal. There is also a link with Manchester City because it was when Leicester City went to the Etihad in February 2016 that most pundits finally expected the visitors to crumble and fall away. Normal service would soon be resumed, most people said. Watch Manchester City crush this dream. Instead, the boys from Leicester, puffed up their chests and destroyed their hosts. And the rest, as they say, is consigned to history – and its imagery.

SRC: I think there was this national feeling that Leicester had been a hare out of the traps and most people said: 'They will not keep that up. That it is impossible that a club such as Leicester City will win the title.' They were proved wrong, of course. And what has been the value of that fact to the British game? In the era when money talks and accountants rule, here is a football club of modest means, but with great team spirit and some key players, turning the world of football upside down. If you could bottle it the queue to buy would stretch for miles. The year 2016 reminded all of us of why we watch the game at all. It gave every football supporter of every aspiring club, at any level in the game, a huge shot in the arm. The moral of this story is: You all matter and one day your time will come. God bless those Fearless Foxes!

'Hands On Head At 1-2' - Manchester City, 2012
(SRC)

CHAPTER 20

There Will Always Be An England

'Worker Being Abused By England Fans' - Bologna, World Cup 1990
(SRC)

'England Fans Being Abused By Italian Police' - Bologna, World Cup 1990
(SRC)

SRC: I was given a luxury campervan by VW to do a road trip to the World Cup in Russia. The British government was saying DON'T GO and no one I knew was going. I drove well over 10,000 miles to be there. Single-handedly. What a driver.

The UK I returned to seemed as alien as Russia and the countries in Europe I had travelled through. This totally took me by surprise. Over the span of 30 years I felt I had come to know my UK intimately through its football, its humour, weather, coast and geography – and its sticking up for others. I had never really felt at home with, or understood at all, Margaret Thatcher, Mark Thatcher, pre plane-crash Farage, post plane-crash Farage, the Daily Mail, Arron Banks, The National Lottery UK etc. etc. Football, above everything else, was how I knew my country and why I began the Homes of Football. Attendances for domestic matches – league games – are still strong despite all the Brexit uncertainty, despite everything. So there's something about being there.

When I am there I never wonder about who they voted for, which side in the referendum they are on. While they might be yelling their heads off in a partisan way, I think THEY ARE FOOTBALL FANS and that is enough for me. Because there's a sort of lore inside the domestic football ground.

But when it comes to supporting Eng-er-land, I approach it with a bit of caution, especially lately. In fact much like I did when I started all this off at the end of the 1980s.

Have we come full circle?

JW: So, let's talk England-on-the-pitch. After recent performances in major competitions you might have got pretty decent odds on England winning the World Cup in Russia in 2018. Last major trophy in 1966 - ancient history. No wins in the group in Brazil in 2014 and then brought down by Iceland in the Euros in 2016. Iceland! Where, exactly, do you go from there? A new young English coach

with a poor domestic club record and little international experience was the FA's answer.

SRC: Ahhh, but don't forget, we actually did quite well back in Italia 90 under Bobby Robson. Gazza's tears and the way we outplayed Germany in the semi-final? I have a little human interest story about Bobby Robson. This was a few years later and he had come to open one of my exhibitions. He was running late, so I asked the gallery manager where he was and he said: 'Bobby's driving around the block – he's a little nervous.' I said: 'Nervous? He's the ex-England manager!' He said: 'Yeah, but it's an art exhibition, it's not quite his territory.' I said: 'Get him in here, he'll be fine, a national hero.' And he comes in and he is very nervous. So I say that lots of people will want his autograph, and he can do those later. I then say:

'Come and have a look at these photographs', and some of them are of England fans around 1990. That young woman in a polka dot dress holding hands with a lad in an England shirt. He asks: 'Who is she?' Well, I didn't know. I just told him that while he was holed up in a hotel in Italy, people back here in England were going absolutely crazy: kids were staying up late wearing England shirts; big parties were happening; mums and daughters and sisters watching matches were becoming England fans, following Gary and Gazza. And now Bobby relaxes a little and he starts talking to people. In the end, we couldn't get him out of the place. He really had no idea of the impact his team had on the country and the England 'brand'. With social media it is probably all very different today.

JW: I was at that World Cup in 1990 with England fans

'Valley Of St.George' -
England v France at Lisbon, Euro 2004
(SRC)

and it was a very weird experience. I started off in Milan and saw Cameroon beat the holders, Argentina, in the opening match. What a start! There was this amazing street party after the game involving seemed like all the Africans who were based in Milan, the street traders and others. It was like a fabulous festival, bringing the whole African continent together but in Europe. This is what the World Cup is supposed to be about. Then, the next day I flew to Cagliari, where England were based. Basically, we had been confined to an island prison, away from all this party atmosphere. Thousands of police officers and press, a thoroughly miserable exercise.

SRC: The real low-bottoming-out-point for England and UK football was in the mid-1980s. We mentioned Bradford and Heysel as tragic wake-up calls. Our England national football-supporting culture was shot through. In Scotland they fared a bit better – their Tartan army were a bit more loveable and so pleased to get to Mexico in 1986.

However, England fans were certainly turning things around after 1990, and by 1996 we had a head of steam on - England hosted the Euros and we had that 'Football's Coming Home' feel-good vibe, a new fusion between music and football. No pop band worth its salt would now claim not to have a favourite football club. No football fan, nor any club, could refuse to turn to music to get an extra kick. Tony Blair was inviting anybody who was somebody to Downing Street for Prosecco. Eng-erland was having a good time, but also showing much more tolerance of others. That sense of superiority and entitlement we once had was finally evaporating.

'Gazza On National Service' - **England At Wembley, 1991**
(SRC)

JW: By the early 2000s we also began to see much more variation in the England travelling supporter; more women, some older fans, even BME England fans going abroad. The England Supporters Group started to isolate troublemakers and to promote a new version of football patriotism. Following England abroad began to feel more inclusive.

SRC: England's home base – accessible for all in the Midlands - eventually did come about, a decade postponed, when St George's Park was opened in 2012. For me, that is the single major recent factor you can identify for why the national team starting to do well again. All 21 England teams spend some time there, women as well as men, and youth teams. This place has facilities to match those anywhere in the world, but it's also pretty accessible. It's not massively security conscious, people can wander about a bit. No guard dogs and sentries. Some trust. I think that is part of the English mentality, we quite like that. So, St. George's Park has that real sense of excellence and expertise, but it also feels very comfortable and really quite open.

JW: With the arrival of St George's Park and discussions about an 'England DNA' it also felt like there was some kind of wider strategy in place for once: 'We don't expect to win the World Cup right now, but we are trying to build towards something better.' At least we had a structure now to hold on to for the future, and things certainly did feel a little more forward looking.

SRC: That's true. We had to move on from Terry Butcher's 'blood and bandages' kind of Englishness. We may, from time to time in history, have to step back from the front of the stage for a while. This was one of those times.

JW: Now we had a plan. And we had a message, which the English public understood, about working with talented younger players, and that bringing them through will take time. We had to try to get away from the media hype that invariably followed England teams around. We were working towards a fresh new approach, no baggage,

The Cure's Robert Smith & Big Country's Stuart Adamson during World Cup, 1986
(Tom Sheehan)

and we were going to work now with younger English coaches, because buying in hot-shot mercenary coaches from abroad had simply not worked. How could they understand us, get the best out of English players?

SRC: The recent successes of Wales and Northern Ireland in international tournaments confirm that point. They have made the maximum out of their national playing base, and Wales certainly have great team spirit but also some world class talent. Perhaps the tragedy of the loss of Gary Speed also offered some inspiration here? Recent successes for England, have probably been a little more calculated than those intuitive ones for Wales and Northern Ireland.

'A Nation's Homecoming' - Cardiff, Euro 2016
(SRC)

'England Fans v Wales' - Lens, Euro 2016
(SRC)

JW: That brings us nicely to the World Cup finals in Russia in 2018. Britain and Russia were hardly the best of diplomatic friends at this precise moment. Of course, Vladimir Putin was going to manage the World Cup finals to the last detail in order to squeeze every drop of positive coverage for his leadership. All host countries do the same. Quite predictably, local homophobia, racism and hooliganism were effectively banished from the tournament under threat of severe state action.

SRC: When I eventually got to Russia in 2018, I found a few English journalists but I couldn't find any other England fans – none. But the South Americans were there in their tens of thousands. They were everywhere: Peruvians, Columbians, Argentinians and Mexicans. In Russia! Sometimes you had to think to yourself: 'Is this really

happening?' It was a bit of a mad joyous dream where everything goes right and not wrong - and you wake up and stretch your toes and limbs and think the world is kind of furry. This is as good as it gets!

JW: The World Cup is becoming a bit of a TV spectacular, which is a real shame, because if you do manage to be there and get among an extreme clash of cultures – a Nigeria v Iceland match or a Saudi Arabia v Uruguay – it is a wonderful thing to be a part of. Whenever do countries like these get to sit at the same table, their peoples sharing a common bond and checking each other out?

SRC: When England played Wales in a rather scruffy French town, Lens, in the 2016 Euros it was equal play. The English were not chucking things at the Welsh or

'The Greatest Throng' - Moscow, World Cup 2018
(SRC)

'Watching England Through The Window' - Kaliningrad, World Cup 2018
(SRC)

'English Car At Nuremburg Campsite' - World Cup 2006
(SRC)

wildly chasing them down the street. They were walking with each other to the stadium, like civilised fans on an equal footing, wanting to see their respective countries progress. In 2016 Russian fans were head hunting and England were the prize. Strangely, in the eyes of the world we were suddenly the victims for once.

JW: It was odd watching the 2018 World Cup from England. Brexit implied nothing was working and as a nation we didn't seem to be going anywhere. And yet, here was a young England football team, with a very young manager (in a waistcoat), which had a real sense of purpose and togetherness. Here was a modern version of Englishness. The parents or grandparents of many of these England players had been migrants. Here was a progressive England, seemingly open and confident of its place in the world, while politicians squabbled over their own narrow, ideological interests. These young footballers in 2018 had a pride and a dignity in playing for their country and they were not weighed down by the shirt or by their national identity. Or Brexit.

SRC: They also looked fabulous, athletic and toned. They were impeccably well behaved. This was not what we were used to, given stories about Premier League players being rich before their time and lacking respect. As England started to have some success I thought I would go back home to see what was happening in England. I thought this is where the atmosphere would now be, that the whole country would be going bonkers, like in 1990.

But there was only politeness, a rather controlled interest. No-one was buying into the media hype this time. Even outside, at the big screens, it was very reserved; people buying and wearing the Gareth Southgate waistcoat was about as wild as it got.

JW: There was not much of the xenophobic tabloid craziness we usually get around England and the World Cup. And people who wouldn't have identified in the past with England and football because of the behaviour of some fans, the tabloid laddishness of the players, or the idiotic media focus on WAGS, could see something different here. I think that really struck a chord. We even had ex-female players on the TV coverage in England. They were not just attractive hosts or eye candy for male viewers. They were offering real punditry and smart analysis based on experience. Alex Scott featured a lot - 140 England caps. She knew exactly what she was talking about, and even if some male panellists tried to patronise her she really wasn't having any of it. Here was another modern shift, a new gender attack to balance up the talkBLOKE vibe.

'Crowd Watching The Big Macth'
- England v Croatia, Weymouth, World Cup 2018
(SRC)

SRC: I think these women are great role models for plenty of younger blokes. The guys were probably thinking, 'Well they're doing brilliantly, they carry themselves perfectly off the pitch and they are doing so well on it.' Those England women are great examples: hard working, no cheating; no running to the press at any moment. Male or female, all ages, I have to say that the national team

'Watching The Big Match Close Up'
- **England v Croatia, Weymouth, World Cup 2018**
(SRC)

players do seem to have equal worth at St George's Park at least – this being the home of the England teams, where roles are defined.

JW: So, is this a new era for England, with male and female teams and age squads developing in concert together? We all know the England women are competitive – they may even win the World Cup in France in 2019. In fact, from nowhere we are suddenly in this incredible position where it's perfectly possible to think that both the male and female senior England teams – and half the junior teams to boot - might win international trophies in 2019/2020. There ought to be right party if that happens! Get The Queen on to it.

SRC: Perhaps popular fandom will flood back to follow these England teams? People like to support success. We probably always knew that we were not the best, which is also why, historically, some England supporters wanted all the flags and noise and to dominate the action off the pitch and outside the ground. Maybe we were starting to think again in 2018/19 that we are pretty good on the pitch, actually. No need to shout the odds or fight the opposition elsewhere.

JW: But we still have that tension in England between the needs of the Premier League and the national team. We have these young players winning tournaments for England in the under-age groups but then getting little or no game time with their clubs. How are they supposed to

develop, gain the competitive experience they need, for senior international play?

SRC: There is a lightly strange angle here that one of the very few possible benefits from Brexit (spits and it hits the pan) is that we might have fewer lower level foreign players playing in England as a result. Ironically, this could give more chances for our own domestic talent. The difference between having a winning national team and one that is just competing is just a few percentage points. Things might be tilting back just a little bit towards the England team.

JW: Southgate certainly has this calm and measured approach to the manager's job. He doesn't look like he's hating every minute of it, as some England men have in the past. It's actually great that this very likeable, ordinary, intelligent English guy is now leading the way for the game. Intelligence has not always been a master trait for the England boss. To lead a very young team to the semi-finals of the World Cup was an extraordinary performance.

SRC: Being out in Russia, one could see that there may be a power shift coming in the international game. Amidst it all, amidst Brexit and all the World looking on us like we don't now what we are doing with anything except the football, perhaps it is England's time again.

'Siding With England v Wales' - **Lens, Euro 2016**
(SRC)

CHAPTER 21

The Homes Of Football By Chance

'Gissa Snog' - Everton, 2001
(SRC)

SRC: Just recently, I heard for the very first time, a beautiful song by the American barfly Tom Waits called, 'I Hope I Don't Fall in Love with You.' I pounced on it. I took it to be about a guy who has a chance for romance with a good-looking woman in a bar, but her bloke gets in the way. In fact, listening to the song more carefully, he did not stand in their way – I was all too ready to blame someone else for cocking it up oneself. Tom's song was

about missing your tilt at the title, in life, because you did not take your chance.

JW: So, taking football pictures at this moment was your fate – this was your main chance, grabbed with both hands. I can see that your pictures can carry so many different messages, just like that brilliant song. You often make us do quite a bit of work as the viewer: 'What's going on here?' The juxtapositions are always really well observed and usually very funny.

SRC: This photograph is of a couple in a clutch having a loving snog outside the Everton ground. The guy is gently cupping his partner's face. One person might look at it and say: 'Oh yeah, it's about a young couple being intimate in public when generally the British are a bit stand-offish'. Another, may think it's a post-match celebration – a special home win. Or are these lovebirds making up – do they even support the same Merseyside club?

My big sister, in a chiding mood, might believe this shot is more about the onlooking photographer, her brother, who is habitually sidelined, always looking on. Perhaps there is a bit of jealousy here, a man wishing for a special someone to go to the match with.

Some time ago now I also photographed a young woman in Liverpool wearing a full Reds' kit and pushing a pram. I intended it as a sideways tribute to a very significant football moment, the dramatic Liverpool Champions League come-back victory over AC Milan in 2005. The Miracle of Istanbul. I took this shot the next day, a wonderfully loyal fan strutting her stuff completely clad in red and who, in my eyes, looked simply great. On social media (Twitter) *Full Kit Wankers* (that's their handle) seized on the picture as if the purpose of the photograph had been to ridicule this woman when my aim had been the exact opposite. I think most people can see the pleasure and dignity in this photograph, but these guys tweeted it as a prime example of what they are about and their guffawing followers (tens of thousands of them) joined in the joke.

There's nothing much I, who produced the photograph, could do about it. Except shake my head and go red with rage. Throw my toys out the pram.

JW: We see what we want to see, hear what we want to hear, even if sometimes all the king's horsemen and all the social commentators in the world feel like they are dragging us in another direction entirely.

I feel sorry for the Twitter men. Not seeing the incredible pride expressed in that particular picture – my club, my community, my place – is a big loss. It's not difficult to ask someone to look at a photograph, but just don't presume they will see what you see, read it in the way that you read it, spot the subtle sub-text. Such is the transaction between the artist and the audience I guess.

SRC: When I came to take each of the photographs in this book, I had all sorts of things swirling around inside of me causing me to seize on this and that, wait patiently for this and that, exclude from the frame this and that, which then changes the way you are allowed to view it. (Incidentally, I never crop a picture once taken and I never fiddle with its colours. So there's no deception going on).

I may have viewed these largely unsuspecting folk in my photos as people who I had seen in my youth, members of my family even. Additionally, I may have recalled old monochrome photographs etched in my mind. I wanted to emulate them in my era, on my watch, in my style and in colour.

Every single time I press the shutter – on old film cameras where it's a slower more reflective process – I feel responsible for the picture. It's like I have delivered a new life. I feel a responsibility towards everything I photograph and everything that is football. My chosen subject.

I don't especially want to be in the football dressing rooms – that feels intrusive – yet I do want to be close to my subjects. I want to have the smells and the sounds of the crowd. The people I photograph often want to talk to me, which is lovely, but can also get in the way of taking the photo.

I use standard vision lenses only so that everything looks exactly how far away it actually was. People have a chance to challenge me, as did that Ipswich Skinhead on Page 33.

I want to have a kind of conversation with my subjects: *I've got a magic little box, you speak to me and look into it – I need you & you need me to make this picture – and that's the magic.* Everybody is clear what's going on and I feel comfortable with that. Yes, it's surely, almost definitely, a conversation between photographer and subject.

Here follows a selection of *My Favourite Photographs*, preceded by *My Most Popular Photographs* gauged from the public reaction over 30 years. The Red Pram lady picture is in this *pop* group – and it could have been in the *fave* group as well.

My Most Popular Photographs

‘*The Homely Fitba Ground*’ – Clydebank, 1989

The boys photo bomb the picture, calling the tune.
If taken today, these cheeky chaps might be cheeky girls.

'The Kop'
Liverpool, 1992

A formidable opponent if crossed.

'*Training Session On The Common*' – Berkhamsted Eagles, 1982

The youngsters play hide and seek inbetween ball practice.

'*Dire Expectations*' – Crewe Alexandra, 1990

*Of the many young hopefuls who set out on the road to
becoming a professional footballer, few will make it.*

'*Neon Girls*' – Tranmere Rovers, 1992

Service with a smile.

'Young Mother Red With Pram' – Liverpool, 2005

*The morning after the night before. She might well strut
her stuff, but Father says the baby remains a blue.*

'Up There In The Gods' – Liverpool, 1990

Doctor Fun addresses his champion fans in their loft,
just off to the side from the noisy Kop.

'Meets His Maker'
Waterloo Docks AFC v Collegiate Old Boys, Liverpool 2015

The goalie concedes one.

'Midland's Semi Final Venue'
Aston Villa, 1990

The classic stadium hosts
CRYSTAL PALACE 4, LIVERPOOL 3!
An epoch changing defeat for the Reds.

'Whereto The Pleasure Of A Man?'
Oxford United, 1990

To the manor born.

'Back Up The Hill' – **Leeds United, 1990**

*The Yorkshire diehards are on a hard walk back
to the top. It's a generation on since they were Champions.*

'Gary Speed Professional Footballer' – Leeds United, 1991

Coming in to his own as a top player.

'*Espying His Likeness*' – Sunderland v Newcastle United, 1992

More than a passing resemblance to...

'*Finding His Likeness In The Crowd*' – Newcastle United at Sunderland, 1992

The Goliath player is body checked.

'A Chicken Is Introduced To The Game' – Blackburn Rovers v Burnley, 2013

Is he about to kick the chicken?

'Splattered Claret Leaves The Table' – Burnley, 1991

It's Fourth Division football for him.

'The Away Lads'
Newcastle United at Ipswich, 1990

The heavyweight champions
of Geordieland, on tour in Suffolk.

'On The Move'
Tranmere Rovers, 1991

After Leyland Daf defeat a few weeks earlier,
the Rovers find one out of two will do.

'*Going Down At Roker*'
Sunderland, 1992

*Flying the flag for the final years at a
historic stadium. A Newcastle United fan
is doing a King Kong on the floodlight pylon.*

'Fog On The Wear' – Sunderland, 1991

A mist hangs around Wearside.

'*Geordies United In The Rain*' – Newcastle United v Sunderland, 1992

Major loft conversion taking place at St.James Park.

'We Live On Oakwell' – Barnsley, 1993

The guard cats Pinky and Perky bunk off their duty
policing Tyke's merchandise.

'Boy Looks Back Going Home' – Barnsley, 1997

*An upward road ahead – hard lessons on a first day's
schooling in the Premiership.*

'*Through Thick And Thin*' – Swansea City, 1994

Small rear garden with football ground attached.
Docile guard dog provided.

'*Shirts On The Line*' – Reading, 1990

Laundry done next door at a reasonable price.

'Peeling Away Up The Road'
Southampton, 1992

Part timers beat the referee's final whistle,
to get an early start home.

'*Looking Up*'
Sunderland v Coventry City, 1996

*Earning their stripes. Sunderland's
brothers and sisters..*

'Home At Shepherdsbridge'
Coniston, 1991

*The locals get their kit off, as
Westmorland League football
returns after the summer break.*

'Welcome To Ewood Park' – **Blackburn Rovers, 1990**

One of the founder members of the League, decked in tiles
and Accrington red brick, sporting reasonable prices.

'*English Premier League Match*' – Manchester City v Leeds United, 1993

*Names and squad numbers are worn
for the very first time, in the top tier.*

'*English First Division Match*' – Grimsby Town v Watford, 1993

Nothing happening on the beach. It's all on the pitch.

'Ticket Office' – **Hull City, 1990**

Levitating shed, platformed on stilts,
designed for the flood of ticket purchasers.

'Experience Surrounded By Youth' – Calver, 2014

The Hope Valley Amateur League team gallantly insists on locals only
- to keep it 'Calver'.

'Looking To Take The Corner' – Buxworth, 2014

*Having warmed up on the practice pitch, the players get their chance
upon their green carpet of a main stage.*

'More Than One Match'
Regents Park, 2015

The super sub warms up.

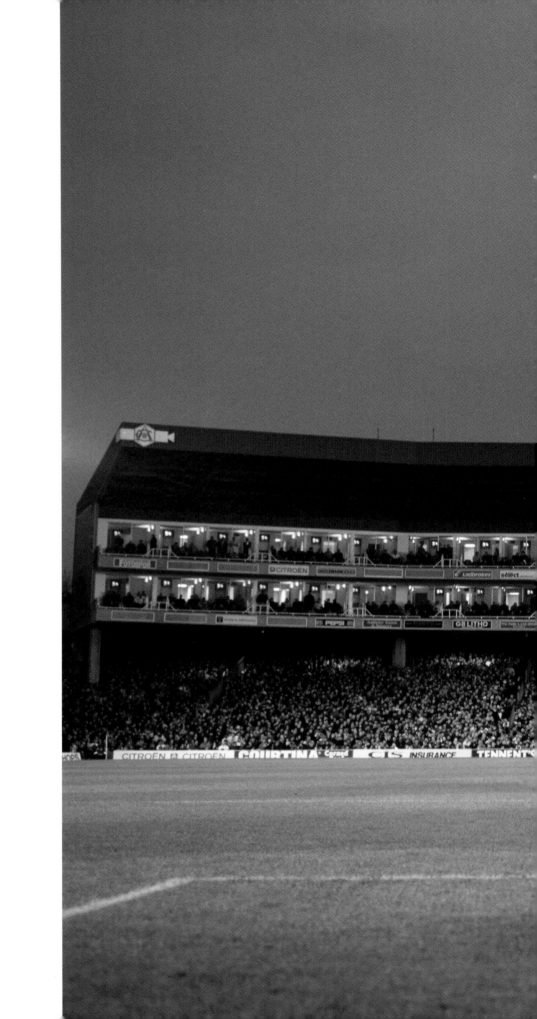

'Higher Noon In North London'
Arsenal v Liverpool, 1990

*Glory of Highbury, Arsenal against
the Champions, under a purple sky.*

'Reporting From The Match'
Wycombe Wanderers, 1990

Motson talks a good game – one that
will not be taking place in this weather.

'*Standing In The Shadows*' – Fulham, 1990

Close encounters of a football kind.

'George Best And Co On The Cregagh Road' – **Belfast, 2005**

Is this the most talented road in the UK?

'Lights On High Over Elland Road' – Leeds United, 1991

The famous diamond floodlights illuminate the encounter with Everton.

'Support From Behind The Goal' – East Stirling, 1996

The hardcore fans. Few were there when Alex Ferguson was manager.

'The Burger Vendor' – Arsenal, 1990

Traditional fayre serving the Hampstead elite.

'*Staring Into Space*' – Hull City at Scunthorpe United, 2007

The brothers are surprised.

'*Sunset Over Springfield Park*'
Wigan Athletic, 1990

The last grassy bank in
English professional football.

'Leeds Road At Twilight'
Huddersfield Town, 1993

Herbert Chapman's old haunt
hosts Southend United in the cup.

'Against The Backdrop Of The Big Two'
Hibernian v Heart of Midlothian,
Edinburgh, 1995

Overseen by Athur's Seat and Salisbury Crags.

'Terracing On Turf Moor'
Burnley, 1990

A million and more people
have stood here, over time.

'The Mudbank Comes Of Age' – Manchester United, 1995

Suspicion is that Scousers are working
overtime at Old Trafford.

'Hillsborough Memorial' – **Liverpool, 1990**

A service is held on Stanley Park, between Anfield and Goodison,
on the first anniversary of the disaster that shook the city to its core.

'*Sea Of Green*' – Liverpool, 1993

The Spion Kop will soon be seated.

'Beneath Beer And Blue Skies' – Nottingham Forest, 1990

The stadium pens will soon be consigned to history.

'Refreshment Kiosk' – Leigh RMI, 2005

Inside... the drinking club are having a lock-in.

'Allegiance To The Wall' – Rangers at Hampden, 1994

The men like to do what they have always done, together.

'On The Bus' – Rangers, 1996

The fans make their way to Hampden.

'On The Bus With The Cup' – Celtic, 1999

The fans make their way to Hampden.
A blue car comes into view.

'What Do We Think Of...?' – Arsenal, 2014

*The club have moved to a striking new stadium,
but the old foe has a familiar name.*

'*Tiara And Tutu Tirade*' – Wolverhampton Wanderers, 2002

They had better win. It's a long haul home dressed like that.

'The Away Support' – FC United at Buxton, 2008

Dogged away support for the people's club.

My Favourite Photos

'*Boy Peers Round The Wall*' – Matlock Town, 2014

*From this position, there is nothing – no fence, no steward,
nobody else much - between him and the football.*

'A Crack At Belle Vue' – Doncaster Rovers, 1990

It was said to be the worst ground in the country. 'A hole'.
But I found a beautiful view. A slither of England's green.

'Yellow Brick Road' – **Bradford City, 1992**

The ground has been overhauled, painted up, made magical.
A scene of shocking sadness just seven years before.

'Chairman In Pride Of Place' – Blackburn Rovers, 1990

A life given to football, captured inside the trophy room.

'Rose In Her Etihad Tearoom' – Manchester City, 2012

*Photographers, club staff, and a wonderwall of stars - Rose has hosted
everyone in her den under the main stand.*

'A Girl Looks Up From The Longside'
Burnley, 1993

The Longside terrace is a coming-of-age
sort of place. A steward checks on his flock.

'The Romance Of Early Season'
Burnley, 1991

Relaxing at a pre-season fixture,
before the serious business begins.

'Waiting On The Men Of Ayr' – Ayr United, 1997

*Mother and daughter, shopping done, brave the torrent
of turning-out-time at the football.*

'*Three Tiers*' – Arbroath at Bo'Ness United, 2014

The generation game.

'Four Lads of South Wales' – Cardiff City, 1994

Did they have a dress rehearsal, or is it synchronicity?

'*Reception Back Hame*' – Kilmarnock, 1997

It's cup final day and everyone is going to Hampden.

'Graffiti In The Shagging Stand' – Dalbeattie Star, 1996

After a match, before a match, irrespective of a match being played,
you can break into the Islecroft Stadium and play your own game.

'*Sombrero Celts*' – Celtic v Rangers, 2008

It's August and everyone is in holiday mood. Irrespective of the score.

'All Along The Mainstand'
Heart Of Midlothian, 1993

The Tynecastle ground has a brewery next
door, and when the wind blows its way,
the stand basks in the scent of hops.

'*Green Eyes*'
Hibernian at Hearts, 2015

*The Hibees fill every seat sold
them for the derby.*

'Kitty In Her Turban Goes Thru It' – **Bradford City, 2015**

A tense sporting service, at Valley Parade.

'Lone Huddersfield Town Supporter' – at Southend United, 1993

His team is struggling in the League with few followers.
And yet, because of segregation, he is made to sit on his own.

'Scoreboard Boys In Action' – Notts County, 1991

*Half-time scores at matches elsewhere are about to be relayed
to the fans here at Meadow Lane.*

'Hereford United v Brighton & Hove Albion' – 1997

*The last day of the season's fixture-list pits
the bottom two against each other. One will go out the League.*

'*Closing The Gap*' – Wolverhampton Wanderers, 1993

Summer allows a window of about eight weeks to tart the place up,
or even make wholesale changes.

'Every Word Of The Programme Notes' – Buxton, 2014

He has arrived at Silverlands early - as he always does.

'*Three Pillars Of Society*'
Belper Town v FC United 2015

*The factory, the church
and the football.*

'Green And Pleasant Landing'
Ambleside United, 1997

*The football forms an integral
part of the Lake District landscape.*

'Welcome To Roker Park'
Sunderland, 1990

*The steps are worn away in places,
from years of support.*

'Boy On A Roker Swing'
Sunderland, 1991

*The lad gets a leg up, above
the eyeline of the perimeter
advertising hoarding.*

'Mowing Roker' – Sunderland, 1990

He plays his part, ahead of the team playing theirs.

'*Viewing Elland Road Together*' – Leeds United, 1990

*It's a lunchtime appointment to view the
valley's cathedral architecture.*

'Best Shirt In The Land'
Dunfermline Athletic, 2013

It's Christmas-time and there's still one left in the window.

'She Wears It Well'
Dunfermline Athletic, 2013

Best be dressed up for the visit of Glasgow Rangers.

'*The Marriage Procession*' – St.Johnstone v FC Lucerne, 2014

*It's early season, July - the team of Perth have a romantic
European date on a balmy Perthshire evening.*

'Face Down Through The Dirty Old Town' – Maidenhead United at Salford City, 2019

Maidenhead have stayed up in the division.
And now they experience Salford up north.

'On The Phone Attraction' – Man City v QPR, 2012

Edgy stuff before the cakewalk crowning.

'It's All Over Now' – Manchester City, 2012

It's all they can say and do at such a time of exhilaration.

'Burst Through The Palace Gates' – Crystal Palace, 1994

Derfying everything he has felt before.
Promotion is his.

'Hair Up, Yelling' – Chesterfield, 2014

Promotion is theirs. The League Two title is in reach.

'*Keeping One's Counsel*' – Chesterfield, 2015

The match isn't going as he would have liked.

'Sisters Gobsmacked' – Dundee at Dundee United, 2015

In the process of being hit for six with hardly a reply.

'Everyone Has To Pay' – Stocksbridge Park Steels, 2012

Checking his customer is getting his money's worth.

'Losing Out To Wycombe'
Kettering Town, 1991

*Kettering's guests have
overstayed their welcome.*

'Birthday Present Time'
Kettering Town, 2015

*Well meant, but met with
bemusement by the players.*

'*Castle And Mound*' – Norwich City, 2004

The fans seeks the highest point to celebrate
their city's highest achievement.

'One Says To The Other'

**'And The Other
Answers The Other'**
Ipswich Town, 2015

*Not everyday you get
to play Norwich City.*

221

'Hanging Out The Washing'
Leeds United, 2012

The men make their way to the game,
going about the houses.

'Set In Stone'
Oldham Athletic, 1990

*Zoe was in the right place at the right time,
to etch her name in concrete.*

'A Photographer Takes Stock' – **Stoke City, 2014**

*The crowd are belting out "Delilah" with its tale of murder; the
Arsenal manager is going ape. The photographer keeps her cool.*

'*Breathing Ayresome*' – **Middlesbrough, 1991**

A town renowned for its chimneys.

'Last Day On The Shelf' – Tottenham Hotspur, 1994

*Everyone has gone home. It's all over for the much loved
stretch of Spurs concrete. It won't be invited back next season.*

'*The Beginnings Of A Forest*' – **Nottingham Forest, 1993**

The summer allows nature to break back into the City Ground.

'Through Their First Winter' – Huddersfield Town, 2018

*Promoted to the Premier League for the first time, critics said they'd be
down by Xmas. But they have kept pace with almost everybody.*

'A New Triumph For T'Town' – Huddersfield Town, 2017

The younger generation never experienced past successes.
They hold their own against the mighty Manchester City.

'King For A Day'
Newcastle United, 1993

The diminutive Chaplin-esque striker,
Andy Cole, is one of the main reasons
the Toon have won their league.

'Date At The Warwick Road End'
Carlisle United, 2017

The most northerly of Football League
clubs enjoys a day in the sun.

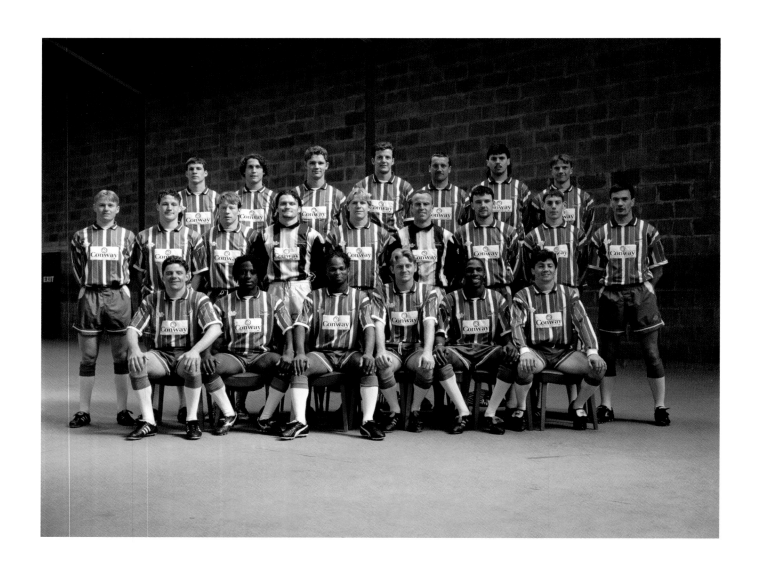

'The Team That Mick Built' – Carlisle United, 1995

*In their deck chair away strip, ahead of an unforgettable
appearance at Wembley.*

'*That Carlisle Jump*' – Carlisle United, 2007

Famous late goals remind one not to leave early from Brunton Park.
A late one against Bournemouth in the fourth Football League tier.

'*Unbelievable Walk*' – Leicester City, 2017

The humble stroll to the ground will never feel quite the same again
after the 5000-1 League title win of 2015-16.

'Ladies Retiring Room' – Bury, 1990

*As the men sit upstairs in the posh wooden seats smoking their cigars and watching
their boys, the ladies are meant to knuckle down to polite conversation and cakes and
ignore thinking about their boys for the span of the match at least. This facility carried
on well out of the Victorian era - and into the 'modern' era.*

'Cry For Home' – Greenock Morton, 1995

*His team has beaten the league leaders in the sunshine. But it turns to
rain and cold - and waiting for a bus which never comes.*

'Days Before The Winter Shutdown' – Derby County, 1992

Talk on the street is of a winter break in English football.
What would we do then?

'The Iron-Man Irony All-Yorkshire Derby'
– Sheffield United v Leeds United, 1990

*The tough player – Vinnie Jones - who has swopped teams and colours
and home grounds and fans, gets it in the gob from new teammate and
gentle-giant Brian Deane.*

'*Night Of Great Expectation*' – Sheffield Wednesday, 2017

*The Kop is full to brimming for the Huddersfield
Play-Off encounter.*

'*Woman In Her Youth Walks By*' – Buxworth, 2014

A shareholder in the community, no less.

'*Stare Off Before Kick Off*' – Hathersage v Ripley, 2015

The visitors are a man short and are quick to psyche out their hosts.
But it will end in crushing defeat.

'Meet You Tonight Down At Ashton Gate' – Bristol City, 1990

*The birds are flying from floodlight to floodlight, which shall soon be turned
on for the cup encounter with Sunderland.*

'Settled In For the Night' – **York City, 2014**

They have bags of something, for their players.

'*Siege Mentality*' – Grimsby Town at Lincoln City, 2015

The biggest game of their season and paranoia is rife.

'*Sincil Goal*' – Lincoln City v Cheltenham Town, 2015

*The Imps are beginning to get their act together
after some barren seasons.*

'*The Spring Encounter*' – Mansfield Town at Notts County, 2019

*The Chairman of Notts has unwittingly upped the ante by exposing himself
on social media. The club who were top the season before, are now bottom.
Mansfield, the visitors, are top and crowing it.*

'Pride Of The Rams' – **Derby County v Leeds United, 2019**

Derby are in danger of being humiliated by visitors Leeds, hot
favourites to beat Derby to the Play-Off Final.

'*Header On Goal*' – Notts County v Mansfield Town, 2019

County, the oldest professional football club in the World,
are under the cosh of their near neighbours.

'Wanting The Shirt Off Regan Poole's Back'
– Newport County at Mansfield Town, 2019

The young girl has travelled up from South Wales for the big match,
to support her Amber team.

'*City Claim The Occasion*' – Manchester City v Watford, 2019

*The FA Cup Final gives the League winners the chance
to add to their honours for the season.*

'Fan Amidst All that Colour' – Manchester City v Watford, 2019

*Watford can't be humiliated (in the FA Cup Final)
with this manner of support.*

CHAPTER 21

Behind The Lens

Desert island musings: how is it I set out to do just one thing for the peak years of my adult life? For 30 years I have awoken at 5am and, for a great deal of those 11,000 dawns, have thrown back the covers and gone in search of the football thing when I could have been pursuing life's other pleasures. Photographing for a living and photographing football especially, sound such fun and hundreds have offered to 'carry my bag' along the way. But alas, I have done most if it on my own and the truth is, it hasn't always been a joy ride, and possibly suiting just the one person.

So the reasons I did all this must be out there – and I propose all of the following reasons put together:

- I was somehow following in my family footsteps
- I grew up immersed in this world of football
- Football had an international language and traversed class and snobbery
- It held a uniquely male index and set of values – something a boy could aspire to
- I could perhaps right a wrong – football itself seemed to be wronged and heading on a crazy course
- Someone had to do it – make a portrait of the national game, in such change
- I just happened to be in the right place at the right time, camera shutter cocked
- I needed a job – other subjects I was interested in would not find an appreciable audience

In the Genes & in the Garden

Can I claim this football mission as being an extension of my family trade? My grandfather Clarke, voted in as an 'independent', held a mayoral role in the 1930s and whilst in office appears to have pursued civic duty rather than 'a political career'. In commissioning sports and recreational facilities he believed he was *doing it for the town*. And what he did is largely still there to see: Butts Meadow football ground is played on most weekends, whilst the open-aired swimming pool (since closed) lives on as a bump in the ground, converted into a skateboard park. As for The Rex – now, officially the finest cinema of any in the country (The Guardian) – it looked like curtains when it closed in the 1980s, but it was resurrected.

Growing up in the family house, between the wars, my dad's three elder brothers formed their own football team and named it after their house: Arosa United FC. My Dad

looked on, as he was too young to play. Then when they went off to WW2, he made the most of his time, manicuring Arosa's pitch, dragging the roller behind the old car he'd taught himself to drive. He was twelve, thirteen, fourteen, fifteen and all along running the house alongside an ailing mother. Waiting for the team to start up again, on his brothers' return – when finally he would have his chance to play in their rank.

In turn, when I was growing up, Dad built a full sized goal in our backgarden. All the kids came round to play. He sacrificed the garden and gardening for balls flying all over the place. All summer and winter we would play in 'the Goal'. It could never be neglected, because we owned it: it was part of our family.

Playing the Position of Observer

My Dad then progressed to helping a youth team and eventually running the entire League. He served every committee role and ended up Chairman. I was party to rearranged fixtures, stop press tales of giant killings, abandonments, punch ups – generally everything which comes with the territory of parents egging on children in sport. I sat on the stairs overhearing his phone-calls – trying to piece together in my mind what could possibly have happened from his side of the conversation, the one

I could hear. Sometimes emergency committee meetings were called and held in our dining room. I loved this world. I knew instinctively that this football pursuit, for all its imperfections, was a rightful thing and worth being involved in.

I rarely got a game for the team I was signed up to, in my Dad's League. I was invariably substitute. I was at the *wrong* school: one that prioritised rugby & rugby ways, over football. My mates still played together at school and quite naturally had a team ready to turn out at weekends as *Berkhamsted Dynamoes*. I could have felt left out. But rather I grew strong – I became the super-observer. A position I retain to this day.

The Golden Summer of 77

It was the summer of 1977 when my Dad as Chairman of the Dacorum Friendly League was asked by Watford FC, through a director who worked for both, if their new manager could be unveiled at his junior football end of season awards evening. The manager was not to be BOBBY MOORE but rather a young guy from Lincoln, a northerner, an ex player retired early from the game through injury. Impressively, Watford Chairman Elton John had personally chosen him.

"Is it alright for him to come along?" came the request. Given that my brother and I would be seated at the head table alongside my Dad, we lept up and said "Boy yes! Can he sit next to us?"

We could hardly believe it when the impressive Mr Taylor (a future England manager) asked us about everything – as if the opinions of a 15 and 17 year old really mattered. Graham Taylor, doubtless held similar conversations with all-and-sundry in good time. But my brother and I were the very first to give our diagnosis and be impressed by the young Watford manager. In the months that followed I presented him with a picture I had drawn of him. He commissioned more pictures to give to his family. Then Bertie Mee, his more famous assistant, ex of Arsenal, got me to do the same for him.

I was bossing it as an artist. *I had a position to play.*

Summer Camp Blues

Having left school and gone to art college, then I went on a summer placement in the USA, to work on a kids camp. The long days were broken up by occasional games of football, however hot it was. Then when we Brits-abroad-together got the chance to play against another kids summer camp, we relished the opportunity. But it looked like it would be a one-off, with no more appreciable time off to arrange another game. Our team captain went to see the Camp Lokanda owner… and was sacked on the spot just for asking. We proposed strike action and more: 'If our captain goes we ALL go'. We got our time off. And a few more chances to become a football team.

At summer's end, the camp owner, looking for revenge, challenged us with his USA-select, in front of the entire camp. He himself would go *in gawls*. This meant that he could wear his fancy hat, not get his medallion pulled in

a tackle, chat to his adoring crowd. With the match at 1-1, and in its final throes, the ball bounced in front of ME who instinctively booted it high towards that sun and towards the goal vacated by the owner-goalie cockily waltzing about beyond his goal area. Amidst stumblings and a cloud of dirt he emerged helpless, clutching his toupee, howls of laughter all around. Possibly the greatest team I have ever played in and the most profound sense of victory I would ever experience.

Hitchiker's Guide

No one could quite believe how I managed to get so many lifts as a hitcher. I even hiked when I didn't need to – when I had my own car in the driveway! I liked thumbing lifts because I wanted to put my trust in other people, and to have them trust me. I am convinced I got so many lifts because I always carried an umbrella. It showed that I cared for myself.

The success of the lifts, which could last hours and hundreds of miles, was in how we spoke to one another. The conversation could always be moved away from awkwardness, if we budged it on to the subject of football. Such talk announced and illuminated which town or city one was from. Some people got teary-eyed in these exchanges, recalling floodlights towering over a hometown they left long ago… huddled folk and extended family, all left behind. I even got a lift in an armoured car and then an ambulance. And, every time, the talk was about football and roots. This undisputed hitch-hiking record of mine: 1300 lifts in a year was against the background of the Miners' Strike of 1984 and continued right up to the time of 'Heysel' and 'Bradford' in 1985. All on Margaret Thatcher's watch.

One day, whilst working in a hotel, in the remote Lake District (I had hitched to look for work there), I was busy with my chores, including clearing out the fireplaces, when Mr Lilley, the hotel owner, positoned himself in the big-backed chair in the hotel communal living-room. Purposefully drawing on a cigarette, he started flicking through the dozen TV channels, his hand extended, a power play. He paused when it got to some news of a fire at a football match "fatalities" – horrific scenes. He carried on puffing, expressionless, flicking through the channels, ignoring my obvious interest in what the BBC was now showing of the Bradford fire. "Bloody football" he muttered, waving it away. I was INCENSED.

Working for The Man

Back in my hometown, I was working freelance for local newspapers of the region. Particularly the *Mail*. One week's roster of jobs included my attending the funeral of a murdered policeman (who in fact I had briefly known over the years). The family, vetting the list of who would be present at the cemetery, was happy enough for 'the local newspaper' to be represented and pleased to learn that I had personally known their Frank. They were adamant that NO national papers should be present – remarking on how *The Sun* and *Daily Mail* had already been intrusive. I felt a responsibility and I went over in my mind my duties for the day in a way I usually wouldn't have done – after-all, this wasn't a local fete or duck race.

I planned the 24 hours ahead: after the funeral I would have the late afternoon and all evening to process the film, make some prints, and deliver them to the paper the next morning. Much like I usually did. No sooner was I home and I got the call from the Hemel office. It was the editor.

EDITOR: *'Those pictures – could you get them over to us, soonest?'*
ME: *'I would prefer in the morning, as planned.'*
EDITOR: *'The plan has changed. Lot of interest in them.'*
ME: *'I haven't developed them yet and won't do until this evening.'*
ASSISTANT EDITOR: *'Can we send a bike over to collect the film then?... we will get them printed up'*
ME: *'Eh?... Er, no.'*
ASS.EDITOR: *'They are needed NOW for A NATIONAL – they go to print TONIGHT.'*

ME: *'But the local paper – ours – was by arrangement with the dead policeman's family to be the only one there.'*
ASS.EDITOR: *'That's why they are needed. No one else has them. An exclusive.'*
ME: *'No, this is wrong... you can't have them.'*
ASS.EDITOR: *'Don't be silly...' (at the same time talking to someone else) '...we can put a few extra pounds your way – the bike's leaving shortly to come to you.'*
ME: *'Well I won't be in! No way. The agreement with the family was just our paper and me!'*
ASS.EDITOR: *(Expletives about me not telling him his business).*
--- Call ended. By me. ---
MY DAD: *'What's going on?*
Situation explained.
MY DAD: *'Stick to your guns.'*
--- Phone rings. ---
EDITOR: *'...Stuart, this is ridiculous. We have made a deal, we have sold them to The Sun! THE SUN!. You HAVE to give over the film. BIKE ON ITS WAY! Name your price!*
ME: *... (expletives).*
MY DAD: *'What's going on now?'*
ME: *'They're threatening to sack me, if I don't...'*
MY DAD: *'Stick to your principles.'*
--- Phone rings. ---
EDITOR-IN-CHIEF OF WHOLE GROUP: *'...Now, Stuart, I understand there has been a little misunderstanding... But you HAVE to do what we say.'*

At 9 am the next morning, as I always did, I dutifully dropped off a selection of prints (but not the negatives). EDITOR and ASS.EDITOR are sat there in plumes of cigarette smoke staring me out. It would be months again before I got another job for the paper – the most demeaning they could find from the scrumpled post-it notes lying beneath their desks. And so it went on, like this, with my being asked to come in and then being humiliated. I had been hung out to dry. I began to imagine working on a larger, long term photographic commission – where I would be the boss and owner of it, without any compromise.

In Football We Trust – Where I Meet John Williams

John Williams was working for the Sir Norman Chester Centre for Football Research in Leicester when I drove up to see him. On an invite. I had read his stuff and thought he might get mine and lo and behold I was off to meet him. In his small office, he peered over his glasses as if he had, in my photographs, discovered a missing universe. A visual Holy Grail. I am over-egging it, I know, but it is exciting to be 'discovered' and see your instinct you-were-on-to-something, validated by a person in office.

John urged that I go on from him and take up with The Football Trust, a body that had money: they were pouring it into concrete projects to rebuild our dilapidated football grounds. And, in his opinion, their rebuilding project lacked a touch of humanity. I had photographs of people using these facilities: grounds built not for one-size-fits-all 'customers' but for humans, with all their faults and idiosyncrasies. John saw a marriage in a kind of heaven for the years to come. The administering authority + the artist = prepare the confetti canon. The 1990's were shaping up to be a glorious time.

The Homes of Football Exhibition & Museum

A simple exhibition grew into a tour (never-ending like Bob Dylan's) and then into a permanent Museum for my work: The Homes of Football At Ambleside in The Lake District. There is a lot of love for what I did there in my 14 years and even now, years later.

One such – exceptional – validation came a few years in to my mission. I get a call from Wads (the team manager):
"It's Wads, I am on the team bus with the lads"
"Good for you"
"And we've had a vote"
"Good for you"
"YOU are coming with us to Spain on the team's end of season holiday, pick you up at 9am from the end of your driveway."

Wad's assistant manager Merv had opted out, preferring to spend time with his family. I got his place. Often one hears that a bunch of lads together can be complete, or incomplete, arseholes. This bunch – Carlisle United FC – turned out to be the nicest, warmest, most respectful, playful bunch of lads you could ever hope for. Along the way I have had little problem falling in love with entire clubs, with sets of fans, with individuals in the game – but now I was a little in love with a team. It made me think other squads might be this special if one got to know them. This was another pointer that I should stick with football as my subject.

Moving Home

Recently, when moving house from 61 Egerton Road which included the garden with the goal – indeed the family home of all of 61 years and where I was born (no one else had lived there before us), I discovered various things in the loft, as one might expect. Old roller skates my sister wore, etc. But in a bound-file marked 'Letters to Football Authorities' I found various bits of correspondence I never knew my father had. He had written to various Shadow/Sports Ministers and MPs. My dad had railed against the football fan ID membership schemes being proposed, post Hillsborough. And I had never known about these letters. There I was, off on my mission to photograph all The Homes of Football with quite a bit of fanfayre, whilst my dad, a modest man, was on a mission of his own. Again I could see how related we really were, albeit a bit diagonally across a table or an awkward silence for much of the time.

And Daughter

SHE, Ava: the beautiful little daughter of *Mr Homes of Football*, had got to 11 years of age WITHOUT EVER HAVING BEEN TO A GAME HERSELF! Moreover, she had never even seen a game on TV. A boy (Dylan) had aimed a football at her in the playground and that is the sum of her footy experience.

Then one day it happened. 'Cleethorpes Town FC', I explain, 'have reached the semi-final!' (I had to explain what constituted "a semi-final"). Cleethorpes is her local town. I then thought better of it and suggested we ignore the fixture and go and feed the ducks/go swimming/go to the eat-all-you-can place/go shopping. Shopping would surely do it. Ava eyes me up, purses her lips and utters those magic words: "LET'S GO TO THE MATCH" We are in the car. "Where are all these people going?" she squeals in delight. She eyes their number in disbelief. She says it looks like a pilgrimage. I say Cleethorpes usually get fifty punters but today it could be two thousand because of the magic of The Cup and the promise of *W-E-M-B-E-R-L-E-Y*. 'They win this and they are at Wembley' I exclaim. There were other things I had imagined my daughter experiencing with me, Dad, for the very first time in her life: flying, swimming in the ocean, discussing the facts of life… seeing a match.

Nearing kick-off, I revert to type: the football photographer, edging us through the crowd to get us

the best viewing position. We crawl through some legs, emerging near the dugout. The 'sponge man', sensing our purpose, or authority, indicates that we can sit on his stretcher. It becomes a makeshift pitch-side grandstand, the best seat in the house – thank you. Driving to the ground I had warned Ava that this would be an arena for swearing – words she might never have heard before or not expressed so forcibly. Now we were here. I pointed to the manager as a central figure in the opera of swearing that would ensue: "If the game is going badly he WILL swear. YES, the F-word. Maybe a C-word as well. If, on the other hand, the game is going WELL, he might doubly swear, out of sheer excitement. In fact, if it's boring he might swear even more, just to liven things up".

There is a goal in the first minute and he's running on the pitch spouting every swear word he has ever known.

One for the Photographers

Should I be training-up an heir to continue to do what I have been doing? Will I ever 'retire'? Is it *too late to stop it now?*

Robert Frank, who revolutionised documentary photography in the 1950's, wrote in 2004 "The kind of photography I did is gone. It's old. There are too many pictures now. A flood of images that passes by, and says,

'why should we remember anything?' There is too much to take in. I am not needed".

My own tactic where I am needed, is to get people to look at more through fewer photos taken – my photos of course – and I try to do this with film, by slowing things down, when the hunger appears to be for digital with its frantic pace.

Desert Island

My desert island was never a desert nor an island but rather in truth a succession of remote or stand alone houses, where I would retreat to and enjoy their privacy and their space. Wherein I could lay out my wares and take a another good look at what I had photographed. Piece together the jigsaw. In the background would be music playing, some songs played over and over again, convincing me that I had merely to provide a visual lyricism to life's great soundtrack, almost certainly *already out there.*

Wake Up Everybody - **Harold Melvin & The Bluenotes**
Someone Saved My Life Tonight - **Elton John**
Rewind The Film - **Manic Street Preachers**
Don't Give Up - **Peter Gabriel and Kate Bush**
Absolute Beginners - **David Bowie**
Just Like Heaven - **The Cure**
Hitsville UK - **The Clash**
All The Way From Memphis - **Mott The Hoople**
Roadrunner - **Jonathan Richman And The Modern Lovers**
Be Ye Mighty Sparrow - **British Sea Power**
I Hope I Don't Fall In Love With You - **Tom Waits**
The Lakelands - **Dean Friedman**
Foreign Window - **Van Morrison**
1996 - **The Lake Poets**
You're The First, The Last, My Everything - **Barry White**

www.homesoffootball.co.uk
www.stuartroyclarke.com

Acknowledgements

Thank you to everyone who backed The Game Revisited on Kickstarter.
Without you, the book would not have been realised.

Amir Alipour-Mehraban	Amy Lawrence
Bryan Armit	Christophe Le Toquin
Buster Baguley	Damian Loughran
Steve Bennett	Anne-Marie Mackin
David Boyd	Norah Maynard
Audrey Branch	Mark McGowan
Damien Brockie	Rod Mearing
Brian Browne	Ben Mills
Mark Bruker	Brendan Moffett
David Cain	Stephen Morris
Gary Childs	Ben Morrison
Neil Coupe	Jon Morrow
The Cravens	Lee & Susan Mullen
Lee Culshaw	Archie Nelson
Stevie Doogan	Ronald Olufunwa
Daniel Edwards	John Oxley
Martin Ellis	Jeremy Patterson
Malcolm Fawcett	John Pietralski
Devin Frank	Alistair Rattray
Stuart Fuller	Relegation Books
Richard Gibbons	Brian Riley
Andy Gilbert	Tim Roberts
Katie & Simon Goodall	Matthew Schofield
Tim Goode	Richard Scott
Joe Gradwell	Nick Smith
Martin Gritton	Craig Spence
Anders Hviid-Haglund	Andy Steele & Jayne Hamilton
Chris Hall	Martin Talbot
Simon Hodson	Louise Telfer
Dallas Hudgens	Sean Twamley
Chris Hunt	George Gavin Tweddle
Patrick Kutzner	Frank Webster
Chris Jennings	Martin Weiler
Juan & Annie	Oli Williams
Thomas Lamm	My Beautiful Game The Film

The Scottish Football Supporters Association

'Joy To All The World'
Liverpool, 2019

*The team has brought back
a European title to Merseyside.*

'A German Manager in England'
Liverpool, 2019

And he is thanked for his contribution.

THE GAME
REVISITED

© Photographs are the copyright of Stuart Roy Clarke
© Archive photographs are the copyright of Mirrorpix
© Foreword the copyright of Hunter Davies 2017
© Texts by John Williams and Stuart Roy Clarke 2018 and 2019

The book came together at:
John's house aside Victoria Park, Leicester
Stuart's Chapel House in Louth, Lincolnshire
Mr G's cafe in Mablethorpe, aside the North Sea

Designed by Ben Clarke Hickman
Published by Bluecoat Press, Liverpool
Printed in Slovenia by Latitude Press

ISBN 9781908457516

BLUECOAT